D0374936

In the Land of
Cocktails

Shake it up!
Laes Brenna

OOgyWaWa!
Ti. Adelaroh

In the Land of Cocktails

Ti Adelaide Martin
and **Lally Brennan**

Illustrations by **Tim Trapolin**

WM
WILLIAM MORROW
An Imprint of HarperCollins*Publishers*

HarperCollins books may be purchased for educational, business, or sales promotional use. For information please write: Special Markets Department, HarperCollins Publishers, 10 East 53rd Street, New York, NY 10022.

Designed by Emily Cavett Taff
Illustrations by Tim Trapolin

Library of Congress Cataloging-in-Publication Data

Martin, Ti Adelaide.
    In the land of cocktails / Ti Adelaide Martin and Lally Brennan; illustrations by Tim Trapolin.
        p. cm.
    ISBN: 978-0-06-111986-6
    ISBN-10: 0-06-111986-5

    1. Cocktails—Louisiana—New Orleans. 2. Cocktails—Louisiana—New Orleans—Anecdotes. I. Brennan, Lally. II. Title.
    TX951.M2855 2007
    641.8'740976335—dc22   2006047090

07 08 09 10 11   ❖ / PHX 10 9 8 7 6 5 4 3 2

**For bartenders everywhere who care about
well-made cocktails.**

We also want to dedicate this book to our beloved city of New Orleans. New Orleanians have shown a courage and resilience even we did not know existed beneath your headstrong joie de vivre. We wouldn't trade being of and from New Orleans for any other location on earth. This one is for you.

25¢ Martini

Contents

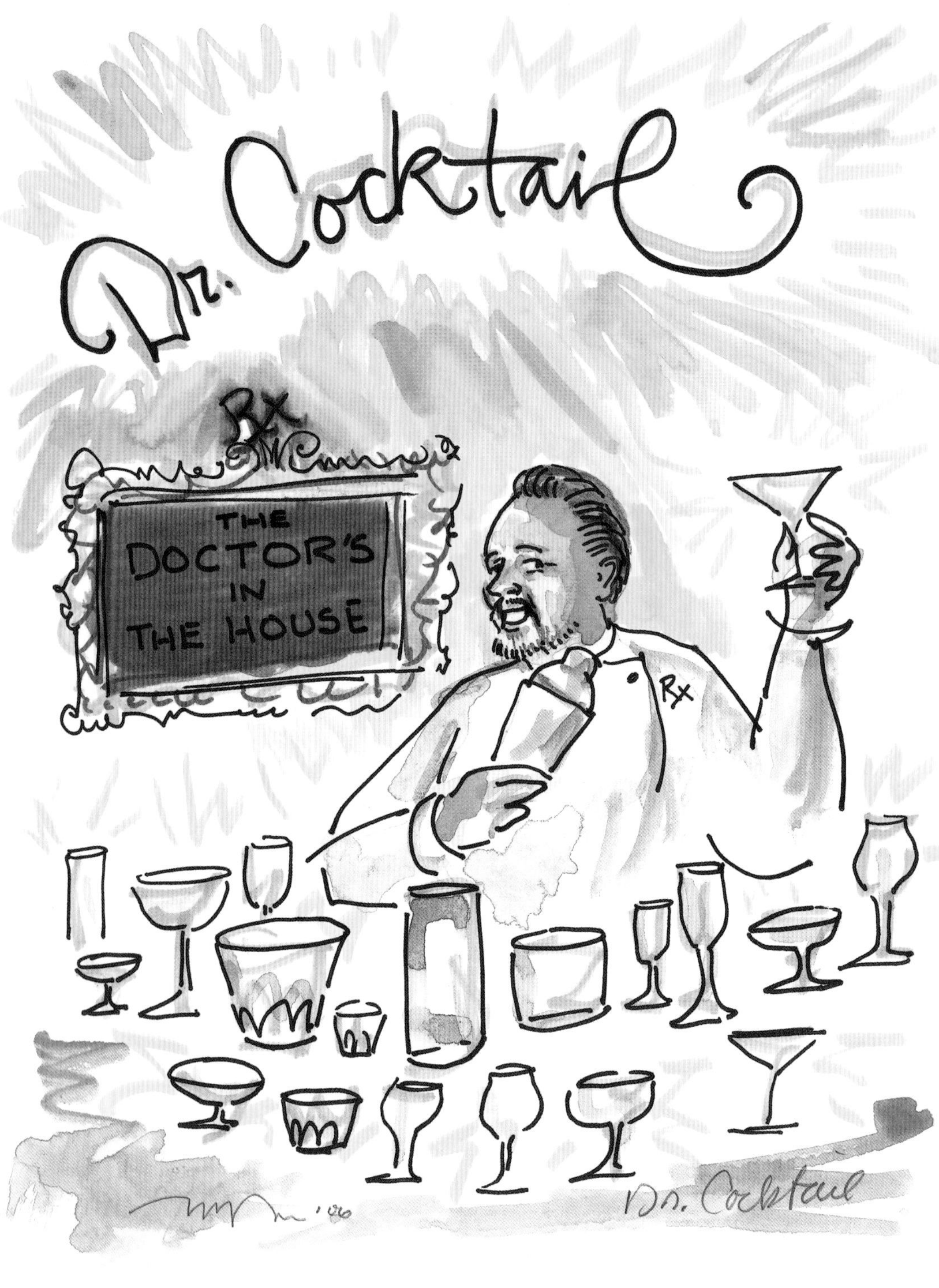
Dr. Cocktail
Rx
THE DOCTOR'S IN THE HOUSE
Rx
Dr. Cocktail

Foreword

Your host chills your glass with ice as he reverently prepares your special drink. You watch as he carefully swirls the green-hued Herbsaint, coating the inside of the glass with faint color. He gravely measures the other requisite ingredients into an iced cocktail shaker, briskly agitating the mixture just long enough for white frost to form on the metal. Into your waiting glass he strains the potion. The pith is carved from the lemon peel to eliminate that extra nip of bitterness, and the peel is twisted with a flourish into your drink. As the first sip kisses your taste buds, you begin to fully grasp the history, the knowledge, the ritual, and the *heart* that go into making your Sazerac, the Godfather of all New Orleans cocktails.

Maybe in other towns they drink rum and Coke or vodka and Red Bull, but here in New Orleans, we drink cocktails—elegant, well-made cocktails. You know that contrary to its reputation as represented by the drunken masses of tourists and revelers wandering Bourbon Street, New Orleans is truly the home of civilized drinking. Yet when away, you find yourself so often disappointed by the cocktails you get, you stick to wine by the glass until you gratefully return home . . . home to the land of cocktails.

Drinking with our guides, Ti Adelaide Martin and Lally Brennan, is always an experience. It's their Brennan blood and their New Orleans heritage. These gals were raised right with both manners and commanding individuality. Take Ti for instance. Tell a savvy local that you know Ti, and you'll get this response: "That Ti, she's such a shrinking violet" with a wide grin that says "Ti Martin: just try and keep up!"

She follows right in the footsteps of her Aunt Adelaide, of whom you will read about in these pages. "Joie de vivre" describes Ti in her depressed moments.

Lally balances her cousin Ti with unfailing liveliness, wit, and warmth, the charms of the old South. One might be inclined to invoke Tennessee Williams when encountering Lally. They both pass my smart test, too: Smart means always getting the joke. And they do. It's easy when you meet them to feel immediately right at home, so gracious are they. Make no mistake, however; with a sixty-year heritage of running popular, sophisticated, and successful eating and drinking establishments, they are restaurant royalty.

Yet these Brennan cousins are every bit as likely to talk about (and to) you as they would talk to and about their celebrity friends, because they love people and they love fun. All the while, they are offering you sublime food and drink.

Cocktails have always been an intrinsic part of the culture of New Orleans. Drinks and food just go together, like laughter and happiness. I remember having brunch at Commander's Palace, feeling a tad guilty at having a Brandy Milk Punch at eleven o'clock in the morning. In came a family. Junior ordered a Ramos Gin Fizz. Mom had Champagne. Dad got a Sazerac, and Grandma went straight for the double scotch on the rocks.

I ordered a second Milk Punch.

You are about to get family lore, stories, recipes, and advice from a unique perspective that can come only from Ti and Lally. Treasure it. It's a given that these two would author their own cocktail book; just a little shrinking violet of a cocktail book—if you know what I mean.

—*Ted Haigh*

Introduction

Make yourself a promise. And while you're at it, make us one, too. The next time you are about to order or make your usual cocktail, order or make a *new* one. You don't order the same dish every time you go out to eat, do you?

You read about food, you experiment in your kitchen, you go to the newest restaurants, you watch Food TV for crying out loud! So why do you keep ordering Cosmopolitans or a scotch and water? There is a world of flavor-packed, subtle, intriguing, silly, serious cocktails out there. You have so much less on the line when you gamble on a new drink—$6 to $11 (even less at home) versus an entrée or an entire meal in a new restaurant.

As in the food world, when it comes to forward-thinking dishes, independent restaurants and bars are leading the way. When you come to Commander's Palace, if you don't try an Absinthe Suissesse at brunch or a Tequila Mockingbird 2 before or after dinner, you are missing out. When at good restaurants anywhere, look at their cocktail menu and ask for advice. We remember having our first Dark and Stormy in a New York restaurant—love at first sip.

As you try new cocktails, inquire and insist that the bartenders use fresh juices and top-shelf ingredients. Ask them to tell you how they are going to make your Old-Fashioned before they make it, and watch them make it whenever possible. Let them know you know how to make a cocktail properly. Then praise them and frequent the establishments that take the art of cocktail making seriously, but still maintain their sense of humor about cocktails—and everything else.

We have studied cocktail making and cocktail drinkers from every angle, and understand why more people don't order or make cocktails. Most of the time, they're *awful*. There—we said it!

Too often the cocktails, made by your own hand or others, are too sweet, too bitter, too strong, just too *too*. Cocktail making is easy to learn but hard to master, because it is all about balance and quality ingredients; balance comes first, and it takes practice. What's more, you have to train your palate to enjoy different cocktails for different occasions or moods. Chances are you didn't like your first sip of wine or beer, did you? You experimented with different grapes and brands. Hopefully you still do.

So what we want to do in *In the Land of Cocktails* is to tell about the history of some great cocktails and stories of how we and other members of our family discovered them. We want to share our culture of cocktails with you. We want you to say, "Oh, let's try a Brake Tag tonight and Champagne Cocktails the next time we have guests."

We share local lore, legends, people, and family stories to put into words how we feel about cocktails, food, good company, and our New Orleans way of life.

As a matter of introduction, here are a few of those characters who enliven these pages: Lu, Doc, and Dale.

Bar Chef Lu Brow hails from Shreveport. She has been with us for several years now at Café Adelaide and the Swizzle Stick Bar. Since the day we met she has proven herself a true cocktailian. Lu believes in the integrity of each cocktail, each time. They must look as good as they taste—and they must taste perfect. Lu lost everything in Hurricane Katrina but was back presiding with authority and an air of naughtiness over the Swizzle Stick Bar before the restaurant even reopened. Lu tested and retested every drink in the book with us; we are forever grateful and we expect our research to go on together forever—all the way to the Saloon in the Sky.

Doc is Ted Haigh, a.k.a. Dr. Cocktail, author of *Vintage Spirits and Forgotten Cocktails*, as well as founder of the Museum of the American Cocktail. We got to know Doc through the museum, but when he ended up living in New Orleans for four or five months as head graphic designer for a major movie company, we became fast friends. Doc's knowledge of the history of cocktails is unsurpassed. His larger-than-life personality is right up our alley, and we think of him as truly a part of our family.

Dale DeGroff is King Cocktail. He developed and honed his extraordinary cocktail techniques at New York's Rainbow Room. His years of knowledge and experience are summed up in his book, *Craft of the Cocktail.* As a food and beverage industry insider, Dale has a pulpit from which he has preached and challenged American bars and restaurants to take cocktails seriously, and to make them well with fresh juices and without shortcuts. Dale and his wife, Jill, are the perfect ambassadors of the cocktail world, along with being cofounders of the Museum of the American Cocktail, and our very dear friends.

Cocktails may well be New Orleans's most important contribution to the world. Would we ever have had jazz but for cocktails? Who knows? But who would want to live without either one? To understand how New Orleans became so important to the development of cocktails three things stand out. Sugar came to America through the port of New Orleans in massive quantities, and was later grown in Louisiana, before anywhere else in this country. Our port was the first to receive absinthe from Europe. Apothecary Antoine Peychaud was busy mixing healing potions, including his own bitters concoction, in the French Quarter. This triumvirate of facts collided in the perfect storm for cocktail history: the Sazerac, the original cocktail concocted of an alcohol, bitters, and sugar syrup.

New Orleans has always been a lively mix of cultures coping with heat, floods, and pestilence. The European and African cultures have histories of celebrating life's occasions with grand meals accompanied by wines and alcohols of various sorts. Cocktails became an integral part of life in the 1800s. The chapters of that history were visible in our upbringing. At home our parents had cocktails before and wine with dinner every night of the week, not just on weekends. We were grown-ups before we discovered that the rest of America didn't do that. And, as a result, we were taught to make drinks at a young age and taught also how to drink responsibly.

We were enamored with the exciting culture of cocktails. Who wouldn't be? The shakers, the misters, the jiggers, the hand-chipped ice, the exotic flavors, the jewel-like liqueurs. . . . We thought it was all chic and smashing—and still do. We have our own collection of cocktail shakers, which we display at our restaurant Café Adelaide and the Swizzle Stick Bar.

Join our revolution and demand well-made cocktails at bars everywhere. We hope this visit to the Land of Cocktails has you mixing, shaking, and stirring a whole new world of flavor and style and fun. And, when in New Orleans, do order a cocktail—a well-made cocktail.

In the Land of Cocktails

We begin our trip to the land of cocktails with a selection of drinks that hail from New Orleans, starting with the Sazerac, the granddaddy of all cocktails. Some are revered, like Brandy Milk Punch, which is de rigueur for Mardi Gras as well as a welcome eye-opener at brunch, and Ramos Gin Fizz, a frothy concoction of gin, an egg white, and orange-flower water. Others are new classics we've created to celebrate friends, family, and our beloved city of New Orleans. The Adelaide Swizzle honors our broke-the-mold Aunt Adelaide. Sometimes it seems that we speak a different language down here from the rest of America, which we celebrate with the Neutral Ground and the Brake Tag. And to show that not even a hurricane will keep us from our cocktails, the Whoa, Nellie! was invented at our first Mardi Gras after Katrina.

 The Mardi Gras crown signifies a drink invented by our group that you won't find in other drink books.

Sazeracs

Lindy and Sazeracs!

Sazerac

Do have just one, as you won't be nearly as
attractive as you think you are after two.

—Ti Adelaide Martin

We are Sazerac evangelists. Perhaps cocktails would never have caught on if the original one—the Sazerac—wasn't such a perfect concoction.

The Sazerac is easy to make but hard to master. As with all cocktails, proportion and balance are important. We've had as many bad Sazeracs as good ones—even in our beloved New Orleans. It should be reddish orange in color. To our taste, Old Overholt rye whiskey or Sazerac are balanced and preferred, and in place of the original absinthe we like Herbsaint, which is not as intense as Pernod or Pastis. We use simple syrup in place of the traditional sugar cube, which most people don't keep on hand anyway.

In the early 1800s the Sazerac was originally made with Cognac and Peychaud's bitters, created by Antoine Peychaud. He named the drink for his favorite brand of Cognac from Limoges, France, the

> Lindy Boggs, a dear family friend, longtime New Orleans Congresswoman, and Sazerac aficionado, was the U.S. ambassador to the Vatican under President Clinton. Lindy lives on Bourbon Street in a magnificent home right in the middle of all the French Quarter action. When Lindy worked in Rome, her daughter Cokie Roberts (famed political analyst, friend, and hero of ours) quipped that it really wasn't that much of a change since her mother was used to seeing men in red dresses.

Sazerac-de-Forge et fils. In 1870, with Cognac harder to come by due to phylloxera in France, rye whiskey was substituted. Absinthe was banned in the United States in 1912, and hence Pernod or Herbsaint was substituted to coat the glass.

As young girls, we were mesmerized when Leroy, the Commander's Palace bartender, held up a glass and twirled it to coat the inside with Herbsaint, the first step in making this classic cocktail.

Makes 1 cocktail

1 tablespoon Herbsaint
1½ ounces rye whiskey, preferably Old Overholt
or Sazerac rye
½ teaspoon Simple Syrup (*page 139*)
4 to 5 dashes Peychaud's bitters
2 dashes Angostura bitters
1 lemon twist with the white pith removed, for garnish

Pour the Herbsaint into a rocks glass and swirl to coat the inside. Discard any excess Herbsaint. Fill the glass with ice to chill.

Combine the rye, simple syrup, and Peychaud's and Angostura bitters in a cocktail shaker with ice. Cover and shake vigorously.

Discard the ice from the glass and strain the shaker mixture into the glass. Rub the rim of the glass with the lemon twist, add to the drink, and serve immediately.

Angostura v. Peychaud's Bitters

There are many kinds of bitters available, but Angostura and Peychaud's are used most frequently in cocktails. Bitters add another dimension to cocktails, much like using the right salt when cooking. Both are made with herbs and spices, including the bitter herb gentian, but each has its own flavor profile. Angostura is earthier, with a more pronounced orange flavor, while Peychaud's is sweeter. Angostura is found on most bars because it is available nationally in supermarkets. Peychaud's is local to New Orleans, but can be ordered online at www.sazerac.com/bitters.html.

Antoine Peychaud brought his family bitters recipe from the island of San Domingo to New Orleans and set up an apothecary on Royal Street. He dispensed medicines but became famous for his bitters, a tonic and cure for stomachaches. These bitters gave an added spark to the potions of brandy he served in eggcups, known to the French-speaking population as *coquetiers*. Soon, those who spoke less-than-perfect French were calling the spiced drink a "cock-tay." Imbibers slurred the word into "cocktail" and the rest is history. The Peychaud's label still reads today as it always has, "good for what ails one irrespective of malady." Now there's a health claim we can relate to, and we can vouch for its veracity, too.

LADIES
NOTICE: WAR DEPT BLACK OUT- 8:00PM CURFEW U-BOAT SIGHTING
OBEY BLACK OUT

Absinthe Frappe

Illegal in the United States, absinthe made from the wormwood plant was said to cause insanity and death. Absinthe is still available in parts of Europe, and it pops up now and again in New Orleans, we hear tell. Drinking absinthe had its own ritual: Some green absinthe was poured into a glass, then a special slotted spoon with a sugar cube was placed across the rim. Water was poured over the sugar, and as it dripped down into the glass, the green absinthe turned a cloudy white.

Today, we avoid insanity and breaking the law by substituting Herbsaint or Pernod, both of which turn from green to spooky white when water is added.

Arnaud's is one of New Orleans's grand restaurants with a storied history, beautiful dining rooms, and a legacy of great restaurateurs, especially the Casbarian family who owns it today. Then as now, New Orleans restaurateurs are the friendliest competitors you'll ever find, helping one another every way we can and having loads of fun together.

During World War II there were curfews in New Orleans; all the lights had to be out by 8:00 P.M. to prevent German submarines in the Mississippi from seeing anything. (Sunken German submarines have been found in recent years near the mouth of the Mississippi River.)

Ella tells us that during the curfew years, Count Arnaud would sneak over to our family's restaurant (then in the Old Absinthe House) after the lights went out and join our parents and aunts and uncles in the ladies' room. It was a large room with a lovely interior and no windows, so the ladies and gentlemen drank cocktails by candlelight, huddling in the beautifully appointed toilette.

Makes 1 cocktail

1½ ounces Herbsaint or Pernod
½ ounce Simple Syrup (*page 139*)

Place a highball glass in the freezer until very cold, at least 30 minutes. Fill the glass with cracked ice. Pour the Herbsaint and simple syrup over the ice and stir vigorously with a long-handled spoon until the glass begins to frost, about 1 minute. Serve immediately.

Ice: The Details Matter

Clear ice, round ice, crushed ice, cracked ice, hand-chipped ice . . . the ice used in a cocktail is all-important. Alex Brennan-Martin (Ti's brother and a first-class restaurateur) has heralded the merits of hand-chipped ice for years. Ice chipped with an ice pick from a block crackles in a drink and takes longer to melt, which is ideal for most drinks. At Café Adelaide there's a large block of ice, delivered from the icehouse every other day, perched in the middle of the bar. We hand-chip ice for cocktails.

Most homes don't have room for a block of ice or an icemaker, so do the next best thing: Crack ice for cocktails.

To crack ice, fill a clean kitchen or bar towel with ice cubes. Place the towel on a work surface, and crack the ice into shards using a meat mallet or hammer.

Between the Sheets

Follow me to Nick's" is a saying familiar to New Orleanians of all ages. Nick Castrogiovanni's Big Train Bar was a serious dive even by New Orleans standards. Each successive generation, including ours, thought they discovered it, and were always surprised to learn that their parents had been there before them.

We grew up with thirteen first cousins and gaggles of friends during a glorious time in New Orleans history. We behaved badly—and we mean that as the highest compliment. We have many blurry memories of drinking Between the Sheets, always popular at Nick's, as a rite of passage during our unsophisticated early adulthood.

Makes 1 cocktail

2 tablespoons superfine sugar
1 lemon wedge
1 ounce brandy
1 ounce dark rum, such as Appleton
¾ ounce fresh lemon juice
¾ ounce triple sec

Place the sugar in a shallow dish or saucer. Wet half of the outside rim of a rocks glass with the lemon wedge, then dip into the sugar. Fill the glass with ice and set aside.

Combine the brandy, rum, lemon juice, and triple sec in a cocktail shaker with ice and shake vigorously. Strain the mixture into the prepared glass and serve immediately.

Ramos Gin Fizz

Louisiana's controversial and charismatic Depression-era governor Huey Long often brought his personal bartender with him on trips to prepare this cocktail, Long's favorite.

When Henry Ramos brought his concoction to New Orleans in the 1880s, he employed a line of "shaker boys" to shake the fizzes to a foamy froth. A customer ordered a drink at one end of the bar and once it was mixed, the cocktail shaker was passed from shaker boy to shaker boy down the bar. The drink was then poured into a glass and picked up at the other end of the bar. People sometimes waited for more than an hour for their drinks. Legend has it that thirty-five shaker boys could not keep up with demand during Mardi Gras 1915.

Makes 1 cocktail

2 ounces half-and-half
1½ ounces gin
½ ounce Simple Syrup (*page 139***)**
2 teaspoons fresh lemon juice
1 large egg white
1 dash orange-flower water
1 drop pure vanilla extract

Combine all the ingredients in a cocktail shaker with ice and shake vigorously until frothy. Strain into a rocks glass and serve immediately.

Vieux Carré Cocktail

The Carousel Bar in the Hotel Monteleone in New Orleans, where this drink was invented, actually turns imperceptibly slowly, which makes for great fun when your friends go to powder their noses and return to find you at the opposite side of the room from where they left you.

We were in our twenties when our parents gave each of us a copy of Stanley Clisby Arthur's *Famous New Orleans Drinks and How to Mix 'Em*, which has been our cocktail bible ever since. This recipe is from Mr. Arthur's book.

Makes 1 cocktail

1 ounce rye whiskey
1 ounce Cognac
1 ounce sweet vermouth
½ teaspoon Bénédictine
2 dashes Angostura bitters
2 dashes Peychaud's bitters

Combine all the ingredients in a cocktail shaker with ice and shake vigorously. Strain into a chilled Martini glass and serve immediately.

The Adelaide Swizzle

We had our very own Auntie Mame. Her name was Aunt Adelaide—she lived life like she was in a movie dream sequence. Really. We're still not sure how she pulled it all off. Glamour and naughtiness all at once, all the time. The stories about her are legendary in our family.

In 2003 we named our newest restaurant and bar after her: Café Adelaide and the Swizzle Stick Bar, because she wore a gold swizzle stick on a chain around her neck. Every once in a while she would lean over and swizzle her drink with her necklace. We loved it.

When we decided to create a drink in honor of Aunt Adelaide, we wanted to use two New Orleans ingredients: New Orleans rum and Peychaud's bitters. And what's the secret ingredient, you ask? Well, we've managed to keep it secret for a couple of years. So, come to New Orleans, taste it at the source, and see if you can guess for yourself. In the meantime, make the Adelaide Swizzle without it.

Makes 1 cocktail

1½ ounces amber rum
Juice of 1 lime wedge
3 dashes Peychaud's bitters
¼ ounce Simple Syrup (*page 139*)
Secret ingredient—when you discover it
Club soda
Lime wedge, for garnish

Combine the rum, lime juice, bitters, simple syrup, and the secret ingredient in a cocktail shaker filled with ice and shake vigorously. Strain over ice into a highball glass, top with the club soda, garnish with a lime wedge, and serve.

Wagner '06 New Orleans   the Adelaide Swimple

Orgeat Punch

*P*opularized at the Roosevelt Hotel Bar, now the Fairmont Hotel, in New Orleans in the 1860s, this unique drink combines almond-flavored orgeat syrup, two kinds of rum, and a few other ingredients. A Creole tradition holds that when visiting a family with a newborn, ladies celebrate with a glass of orgeat syrup only, while the gentlemen drink orgeat punch in honor of the household's new angel.

What's orgeat syrup? Made from almonds, sugar, and rose or orange-flower water, its distinctive almond taste adds an alluring flavor to many cocktails. Look for Torani or Monin brands.

Makes 1 cocktail

1½ ounces spiced rum, such as Captain Morgan
1 ounce orgeat syrup
½ ounce 151 proof rum, such as Bacardi
½ ounce limoncello
½ ounce fresh lemon juice
½ ounce fresh lime juice

Combine all the ingredients in a cocktail shaker with ice. Pour the contents of the shaker, including the ice, into a highball glass. Top off the drink with additional ice and serve immediately.

When our parents were in their twenties, they ran a restaurant in the French Quarter and decided to sell lunchtime Martinis for 25¢, a bargain even in those days. Those Martinis certainly helped put the restaurant on the map.

Fast-forward to about 1999. Aunt Dottie kept telling us that we should do the same at Commander's Palace, repeating her message like a broken record. We told her people didn't drink like that in the daytime anymore, the world was too fast-paced, etc. We finally caved in, mostly so we would stop hearing about it.

Wrong, wrong, wrong—we were so wrong. It took about a year for word to spread about our bargain lunchtime cocktail, but when it did—wow! We developed four different Martinis in four different colors, even an aqua blue one to match the Commander's Palace exterior.

Any weekday when you walk into the Commander's Palace dining room, there will be brightly colored drinks on many tables. People celebrating that the Saints won a game, or their child finally graduated, or—well, our locals never need much of a reason.

We now listen to Aunt Dottie more often.

Ray's Melon Martini ♛

Witty, ultraprofessional, and an expert at twirling a glass with Herbsaint for a Sazerac into the air, our dear friend and maestro of Commander's dining room, Ray Brinkman has the world's greatest laugh—and uses it often. Ray loved our 25¢ Martini schtick and, as usual, was not to be left out, so he invented this one to add to the array of our brightly colored Martinis.

Makes 1 cocktail

2 teaspoons superfine sugar
1 lemon wedge
2 ounces vodka
¾ ounce Sour Mix (*page 139***)**
½ ounce Midori
1 maraschino cherry

Place the sugar in a shallow dish or saucer. Wet half of the outside rim of a rocks glass with the lemon wedge and dip into the sugar. Fill the glass with ice and set aside.

Combine the remaining ingredients, except the cherry, in a cocktail shaker filled with ice and shake vigorously. Strain into the glass with the ice, garnish with the cherry, and serve immediately.

Commander's Palace Martini

The exterior of Commander's Palace is painted a shocking blue-green aqua color. Our Aunt Adelaide and her decorator, Charlie Gresham, wanted to send a message to New Orleans that the Brennan family had taken over the place and things were going to get exciting. If you go to a paint store in New Orleans, you can ask for Commander's Blue, the same color as this Martini.

Makes 1 cocktail

2 tablespoons superfine sugar
1 lemon wedge
2 ounces vodka
½ ounce Sour Mix (*page 139*)
½ ounce blue curaçao
2 lemon wedges, squeezed and dropped into the shaker
Splash of Sprite
Lemon twist, for garnish

Place the sugar in a shallow dish or saucer. Wet half of the outside rim of a rocks glass with the lemon wedge and dip into the sugar. Fill the glass with ice and set aside.

Combine the remaining ingredients, except the lemon twist, in a cocktail shaker filled with ice and shake vigorously. Strain into the prepared glass, garnish with the lemon twist, and serve.

Saloon in the Sky

Jazz funerals in New Orleans celebrate the deceased's life with dancing and singing to commemorate a loved one's ascendance to heaven. As children, we often heard about the saloon in the sky, an invention of Ella's, where all the people she loves (and no one that she doesn't) are sitting around a piano, eating and drinking and carrying on. The bar looks like the one she and her siblings ran in the 1950s, the Old Absinthe House on Bourbon and Bienville in the French Quarter. Fats Pichon is playing. Louis Armstrong and Ella Fitzgerald are singing. The food is great, the drinks are better, and the company perfect.

"You think of the afterlife however you want," says Ella. "For me, it's the saloon in the sky."

So, at the saloon in the sky there are no hangovers, and a drink tastes like a drink.

Makes 1 cocktail

1 ounce Maker's Mark
½ ounce applejack or apple brandy
½ ounce Grand Marnier

Combine all the ingredients in a cocktail shaker and shake vigorously. Strain the cocktail into a rocks glass, add ice to fill, and serve.

Neutral Ground ♕

We both went to college in Texas, and that was the first time we ever heard a bartender announce last call (foreign to us New Orleans kids), or someone call the grassy strip in the middle of an avenue a median. In New Orleans a street median is called neutral ground. The original neutral ground on Canal Street served at one time as the divider between the French Vieux Carré (now the French Quarter) and the American sector just across the street to the north. It became the spot where commerce could be done without one group's having superiority over the other—completely neutral.

Since 2005, this drink has been popular at Café Adelaide and the Swizzle Stick Bar—both neutral spots for all concerned parties.

Makes 1 cocktail

1½ ounces limoncello
1½ ounces peach schnapps
1 ounce Sour Mix (*page 139*)

Combine all the ingredients in a cocktail shaker with ice and shake vigorously. Strain into a chilled Martini glass and serve immediately.

Top Shelf or Well?

Top-shelf spirits are the brand-name bottles you see when sitting at a bar. Well bottles refer to those no-frills brands that are usually kept below the bar within reach of the bartender. Order a scotch and soda and you'll get a no-name well brand. Ask for Johnny Walker Red and you'll get that specific top-shelf scotch.

In some of our cocktail recipes, we call for specific top-shelf spirits and liqueurs, because their flavor profiles result in properly balanced drinks. For instance, Maker's Mark is called for in the Whiskey Smash because it imparts just the right clean, light smoothness that Dale DeGroff says this cocktail requires. Sure you can use another bourbon, but we encourage you to try the specific spirits and liqueurs suggested—they will make all the difference.

Whoa, Nellie! ♛

The scene: Mardi Gras 2006, the first one after Hurricane Katrina. We're at Lally's house on the parade route with friends, family, and all sorts of characters, Doc Cocktail Ted Haigh among them. Lally's in the mood to create a new drink; she enlists Doc to help. Our CFO and good-time gal Arlene Nesser is not to be left out. After many false starts, lots of scrunched-up faces, and "oh gross"es, divine inspiration then intervened (with a dose of Doc's knowledge about balance) and a classic was born. After his first sip, he said, "Whoa, Nellie!" Nellie Valentine being our grandmother's name, it stuck—both the drink and the name!

We make this with locally produced Sazerac rye, because it's only right, but another brand of rye can be used.

Makes 1 cocktail

1¼ ounces Sazerac rye or other rye
¾ ounce dark rum, such as Myers's
¾ ounce Cointreau
4 dashes Angostura bitters
½ ounce fresh lemon juice
½ ounce grapefruit juice
½ ounce Simple Syrup (*page 139*)

Fill a Martini glass with ice and set aside to chill. Combine all the ingredients in a cocktail shaker with ice and shake vigorously. Discard the ice from the glass. Strain the drink into the glass and serve immediately.

Brake Tag

When Ti moved away from New Orleans for the first time, a cop pulled her over and told her the inspection sticker had expired. Ti said, "What's that?" No getting out of that ticket. In New Orleans, we call inspection stickers "brake tags." You might want to put the brakes on after just one of these, but it's a good way to kick-start a summer evening.

Makes 1 cocktail

1 ounce Southern Comfort or other bourbon
1 ounce amaretto
1 ounce orange juice
1 ounce cranberry juice
1 orange wedge
1 maraschino cherry

Combine the bourbon, amaretto, and orange and cranberry juices in a cocktail shaker with ice and shake vigorously. Strain the cocktail into a highball glass filled with ice. Skewer the orange wedge and cherry on a cocktail pick, place in the glass, and serve immediately.

For many years, Anne Rice was our neighbor near Commander's Palace. People walked in the door of the restaurant only wanting to know where the writer lived. We particularly love it when she writes about our local cemetery, the one across the street called Lafayette Cemetery #1. "We're across the street from the dead center of New Orleans," our Uncle Dick loved to say.

One day Anne Rice arrived at the cemetery in a coffin in a horse-drawn carriage followed by hoards of fans. Just another day in the neighborhood.

Whiskey Smash

We'll probably be run out of the South, but we think this is an improvement on the Mint Julep. The lemon tames the mint so it does not overwhelm the drink as it can in a julep. It was invented by King Cocktail himself, our friend Dale DeGroff.

Makes 1 cocktail

3 lemon wedges
4 fresh spearmint leaves
1 ounce orange curaçao
2 ounces Maker's Mark
1 sprig fresh spearmint

Muddle the lemon wedges, mint leaves, and curaçao in a bar glass. Add the bourbon and ice and shake well. Strain the drink into a rocks glass filled with ice and garnish with the mint sprig. Serve immediately.

No matter how fabulous we think our cocktail list is, most folks stick to their usual Martini or scotch on the rocks. They never order a Corpse Reviver Number 2 or even a Sidecar—until we send out a Trouble Tree.

When you sit down for dinner at Commander's Palace or Café Adelaide, one of our team might appear with three to seven shot glasses hanging from a metal tree of sorts. The cocktail samples in front of you are explained as you taste a real Daiquiri or a Cachaça Swing or a French 75. This is a perfect way to sample the best cocktails in town.

Classic
Cocktails

When our family traveled together, perhaps to New York, Los Angeles, Paris, or Monte Carlo, the adults would meet in the hotel bar before dinner.

We were always ready first, so we'd go to the bar to wait for our parents and aunts and uncles while they dressed. Oh, we thought, growing up is going to be grand if being a grown-up is like this. Then they would make an entrance, the women sometimes wearing hats, but more often gloves—long ones on occasion that they'd make a show of undoing, only to leave the last pearl button snapped closed and the glove dangling. This so they could reach into their evening bags for cigarettes from velvet-lined cigarette cases with their latest initials. They didn't carry matches or lighters, because there was always a gentleman there to light their cigarettes.

Then they ordered cocktails—Sazeracs and Stingers and Martinis and Scotch Old-Fashioneds. Their manners were impeccable, and their personalities full-flavored. They loved it when someone leaned in and whispered a salty story. They'd laugh, heads back, cigarettes in a long, long filter in one hand and a cocktail in the other.

Hot, Hot and Dirty Martini ♛

Here's an example of what a flavored rim can do to a traditional cocktail like the Martini. Sweet paprika is used here, but a zesty Hungarian paprika will give the drink a good kick.

Makes 1 cocktail

1 teaspoon sweet paprika
1 teaspoon salt
1 teaspoon cayenne pepper
1 lemon wedge
2 ounces vodka
½ ounce olive brine

Place the paprika, salt, and cayenne pepper on a saucer and mix together with a fork. Wet half the rim of a chilled Martini glass with the lemon wedge and dip into the seasoning mix. Set aside. Combine the vodka and olive brine in a cocktail shaker with ice and shake vigorously. Strain into the prepared glass and serve immediately.

Salted or Sugared Rims

Salted or sugared rims look pretty and add another layer of flavor to many drinks, but a little goes a long way. Our practice is to salt or sugar (or cayenne) just half the rim, so there are options for each sip. Just wet half of the rim with the appropriate fruit juice before dipping in a saucer of salt, sugar, or cayenne.

Shaken v. Stirred

Our apologies to James Bond, but a Martini should be stirred, not shaken. Any drink with clear ingredients should be left as pure as possible. Don't fiddle with it. When you add liqueur, juice, or cream to a cocktail, then shake away.

Margarita

Since we went to college in Texas, need we say more about our familiarity with and affection for Margaritas? We knew where to get the best, the cheapest, and the biggest Margaritas in Dallas. One place served three-for-one Margaritas whenever it rained, which did nothing for class attendance at SMU.

Our cousin Brenne, who also went to SMU with us, would throw New Orleans–inspired parties with extraordinary food and amazing Margaritas. Brenne came home from college with a degree and a Margarita machine.

Tequilas are available in four categories with a wide range of prices. Blanco (silver) is clear, strong tequila bottled straight from the distillery, the stuff for drinking shots. Oro is gold in color as its Spanish name says and is used in mixed drinks, including Margaritas. Pale in color, Reposado is blanco that has been aged, or rested, for at least two months. Añejo tequila is aged in oak casks for one to many years, and like fine Cognac is best when slowly sipped.

Makes 1 cocktail

2 tablespoons kosher or sea salt
2 lime wedges
1½ ounces Blanco tequila
¾ ounce Cointreau or triple sec
1 ounce fresh lime juice
¼ ounce Simple Syrup (*page 139***)**

Put the salt in a saucer. Rub half of the rim of a Margarita or a Martini glass with 1 lime wedge. Dip the rim into the salt. Using a clean cloth, wipe any excess salt from inside the glass and set aside.

Combine the tequila, Cointreau, lime juice, and simple syrup in a cocktail shaker filled with ice and shake vigorously. Strain into the prepared glass and garnish with the remaining lime wedge. Serve immediately.

Lemons and Limes

Lemons and limes vary in their flavor and acidity. Taste your fruit juice before making cocktails so you will know how to balance the drinks. Also know that the older the fruit or the longer it sits after being cut, the stronger the flavor.

Whiskey Cocktail

According to Ted Haigh, this cocktail, which dates to the early 1800s, is the forerunner to many whiskey-based drinks, including Doc's favorite, the Old-Fashioned (*page 37*).

Makes 1 cocktail

3 ounces Sazerac rye or other rye whiskey
2 dashes orange curaçao
1 dash Simple Syrup (*page 139*)
2 dashes Angostura bitters

Combine the ingredients in a rocks glass and stir. Add enough ice to come half to three-quarters of the way up the sides of the glass. Serve immediately.

Muddling

Muddling means to mash or crush an ingredient to release its flavor, such as the mint in a Mint Julep or the orange and cherry in an Old-Fashioned. There's even a specific piece of equipment called a muddler, designed for getting around the bottom of the glass, while its larger end is meant to fit in the palm of your hand. A long-handled spoon will do the trick. Leave the muddled mint leaves or fruit large enough so that the pieces don't get sucked up and stuck in your straw.

Muddled drinks often call for a sugar cube rather than simple syrup. The grittiness of the sugar provides some traction, making it easier to release essential oils from the herb leaves or citrus fruit.

Old-Fashioned

An Old-Fashioned can be made with muddled orange and cherry or with muddled orange peel only. In the first version, here, the orange section is muddled with sugar to release the essential oils in the orange peel.

Makes 1 cocktail

1 orange slice
1 maraschino cherry
1 sugar cube or 1 teaspoon granulated sugar
3 dashes Angostura bitters
1½ ounces bourbon
1 ounce club soda

Muddle together the orange, cherry, and sugar in the bottom of a rocks glass. Add the bitters and bourbon, and stir well. Add ice to fill the glass halfway and top off with the club soda. Serve immediately.

Doc's Favorite Old-Fashioned

Lu says it's important to use Sazerac rye whiskey in this drink, and who are we to disagree? Not only does it impart a unique flavor but also it's made in New Orleans! Cheers to a native cocktail!

Makes 1 cocktail

**1 large orange peel,
about 2 x 2 inches, scraped to
remove as much pith as possible
6 to 8 drops Angostura bitters
1 sugar cube
3 ounces Sazerac rye whiskey**

Place the orange peel, bitters, and sugar in a rocks glass and muddle. Add the whiskey, stir, and add enough ice to come halfway to three-quarters of the way up the sides of the glass. Serve immediately.

Scotch Old-Fashioned

There are many schools of thought when it comes to the Old-Fashioned. You can muddle the fruit or not. You can make it with bourbon, rye whiskey, brandy, rum, or scotch, as in this recipe. We're from the muddling school, and muddling in the same glass you're going to drink from. A sacrilege, some say. Well, you get to an age where you have set opinions on life's big questions.

Some years back, Ella Brennan (Ti's mother) was recovering from a brief illness. Up until this point, she drank, for the most part, only wine for many years. We knew we had entered a new phase in her recovery when she said, "I'll have a Scotch Old-Fashioned." All of us at the table burst into surprised laughter—Mom was back and kicking up her heels!

Makes 1 cocktail

1 orange slice
1 maraschino cherry
1 sugar cube or 1 teaspoon granulated sugar
3 dashes Angostura bitters
1½ ounces scotch
1 ounce club soda

Muddle together the orange, cherry, and sugar in the bottom of a rocks glass. Add the bitters and scotch, and stir well. Add ice to the glass and top off with the club soda. Serve immediately.

Brandy Crusta

When the Museum of the American Cocktail opened in 2005, it was a perfect New Orleans day for a party on a French Quarter patio. The banana trees were gently swaying and a faint river breeze welcomed the ambassadors of the cocktail. Multiple founders of the museum, including master bartender Dale DeGroff, were on hand serving drinks. Dale, by sheer force of will and personality, has made America realize that there is a difference between a drink and a well-made drink.

We were delighted to be served Brandy Crustas because the drink was invented in New Orleans circa 1852 by Joseph Santina at the Jewel of the South on Gravier Street. Ted Haigh proposes that the oft-forgotten Brandy Crusta was the predecessor to the ubiquitous Sidecar.

The garnish for this drink is nearly the entire peel from one lemon. To make this dramatic garnish, slice off the top and bottom ends from one medium lemon. Starting at one end, carefully slice away the lemon peel with a knife, keeping it as whole as possible. It's okay if there's still a bit of the white pith attached.

Makes 1 cocktail

Peel from 1 lemon
2 tablespoons superfine sugar
1 lemon wedge
1½ ounces domestic brandy
¼ ounce maraschino liqueur
¼ ounce Cointreau
¼ ounce fresh lemon juice

Place the lemon peel in a small stemmed cocktail or sherry glass. Place the sugar in a shallow dish or saucer. Wet half of the outside rim of the glass with the lemon wedge and dip into the sugar. Wipe the inside of the rim, leaving the sugar on the outer rim, and set aside.

Combine the remaining ingredients in a cocktail shaker with ice and shake vigorously. Strain into the prepared glass and serve immediately.

Balance

If we've learned anything about cocktails, it is that a good cocktail is all about balance. It's easy for any drink that has more than three, four, or more ingredients to lose its equilibrium and become off balance.

Any cocktail can taste different from one time to the next. Perhaps the limes are less tart than usual, or the simple syrup isn't as sweet, or the brand of rum used has a different flavor from the one you're used to. We suppose if you always drink the same brand of scotch and water, you're okay. But gee, why'd you buy this book then?

Taste and adjust your drinks every time you make them.

Gin Gimlet

'll have a Gimlet, please." We like the way it sounds—like a real drink. We always preach about using fresh juice in cocktails, but the Gimlet is best when made with Rose's bottled lime juice. When made with fresh lime juice, this is an entirely different drink.

Makes 1 cocktail

2 ounces gin
1 ounce Rose's lime juice

Combine the gin and Rose's lime juice in a rocks glass. Fill the glass with ice and stir. Serve immediately.

After a particularly amateurish night of indulging, Ti's mother, Ella, inquired about what she had drunk. When Ella learned that wine, scotch, and beer were involved, she lectured Ti about not mixing the grain and the grape, a rule taught to New Orleans youth by their parents. Drinking is a part of life in New Orleans, and one is expected to learn to do it well. Hangovers are a drag and a waste of time. Getting drunk is so unattractive. Avoid it all by picking one thing to drink for the evening and sticking to it. One cocktail before dinner followed by wine can be handled, but mixing it up back and forth all night is a surefire recipe for the vapors.

The Vapors

Whenever we asked our Aunt Adelaide why she was always waving around a slightly damp handkerchief in front of her face, she said she had "the vapors." When we inquired what the vapors were, she said it was kind of like a headache. Now, it seemed strange to us as young girls that waving a wet hanky around would have any curative value, but then Aunt Adelaide was unlike anyone else.

A few years ago, writer and dear family friend Peter Feibleman asked Ti if she knew what was in the curious vapors remedy. When she said she only remembered the wafting of the handkerchief, he wrote down the recipe on a napkin. Turns out Aunt Adelaide's remedy was four parts ethyl alcohol, one part ether, and a few drops of a favorite perfume. Who knew that she had a lady pharmacist in a certain New York pharmacy who dispensed ether, the key ingredient in her hangover remedy? Not only would Aunt Adelaide soon feel better but you could operate on her, too!

Sweet Cream

Sweet cream, essentially lightly sweetened cream, is no longer available, so you need to make your own. In a small glass or jigger, combine ½ ounce heavy cream and ¼ teaspoon sugar, stir well to dissolve the sugar, and measure out the amount called for in a drink.

Gin Rickey

This drink reminds Lally of a crisp white linen suit in summer. Most refreshing.

Makes 1 cocktail

1½ ounces gin
Juice from 1 lime wedge
2 ounces club soda

Combine the gin and fresh lime juice in a highball glass. Fill the glass with ice, top with the club soda, and stir. Serve immediately.

Whiskey Sour

We always love classic, simple things: dresses, dishes, and drinks. You may remember this as the first drink you were ever offered. Classic, yet simple.

Makes 1 cocktail

2 ounces bourbon
1 ounce fresh lemon juice
½ ounce Simple Syrup (*page 139*)

Combine all the ingredients in a cocktail shaker with ice and shake vigorously. Strain the drink into a rocks glass and top with ice. Serve immediately.

Corpse Reviver Number 2

Here is another classic cocktail from the 1930s, for which there are many versions. This features Lillet, a French wine-based aperitif. We also use a few drops of Herbsaint in place of the traditional absinthe.

This refreshing summertime drink is also pretty to look at in its stemmed cocktail glass with the cherry at the bottom.

Makes 1 cocktail

1 ounce Tanqueray or Bombay gin
1 ounce Cointreau
1 ounce fresh lemon juice
1 ounce Lillet blanc
3 drops Herbsaint, Pernod, or Ricard
1 maraschino cherry without stem

Fill a Martini glass with ice to chill. In a cocktail shaker with ice, combine the gin, Cointreau, lemon juice, and Lillet and shake vigorously. Strain the cocktail into the glass.

Insert a plastic straw into the Herbsaint bottle and draw a small portion of the liqueur into the straw by placing your finger on the top of the straw. Withdraw your finger slowly and tap the straw three times to extract about 9 small drips, or the equivalent of 3 large drops, into the drink.

Sink the cherry to the bottom of the glass and serve immediately.

'06 New Orleans

Corpse Reviver

Lemon Drop

$\mathcal{R}$emember lemon drop candies? Well, this tastes the same, only with a kick.

In New Orleans, there's an Italian ice cream parlor/pastry shop called Brocato's, now run by the third generation of the family. This cocktail tastes just like the lemon ice they make during warm weather months, and is equally refreshing. Our Aunt Dottie is fond of anything that approaches the lemony flavor of her beloved lemon icebox pie, especially if it is pretty and has vodka in it.

Makes 1 cocktail

2 tablespoons superfine sugar
2 lemon wedges
1 ounce lemon- or citron-flavored vodka
1 ounce limoncello

Place the sugar in a shallow dish or saucer. Wet half of the inside and outside rims of a chilled Martini glass with one of the lemon wedges and discard the wedge. Dip the rims into the sugar and set aside.

Combine the vodka, limoncello, and juice from the remaining lemon wedge in a cocktail shaker with ice and shake vigorously. Strain into the prepared glass and serve immediately.

Sidecar Number 1

Suffering from a chill from riding in a motorcycle sidecar, a World War I officer asked a bartender for a warming drink. Derived no doubt from the Brandy Crusta invented in New Orleans in the mid-eighteenth century, the Sidecar was most likely invented in Paris. Lu's advice to the uncertain: "This is a big beautiful drink for a connoisseur of cocktails." We're on a mission to help revive this fabulous old cocktail!

It's made with domestic brandy rather than the usual Cognac and has a lighter mouth feel. If you prefer a bolder taste, substitute Cognac for domestic brandy and a touch more fresh lemon juice for what Lu calls "the perfect Sidecar."

Makes 1 cocktail

2 tablespoons superfine sugar
1 lemon wedge
2 ounces domestic brandy
1 ounce Cointreau
½ ounce fresh lemon juice
1 lemon twist

Place the sugar in a shallow dish or saucer. Wet half of the inside and outside rims of the glass with the lemon wedge and discard the wedge. Dip the rims into the sugar. Fill the glass with ice and set aside.

In a cocktail shaker with ice, combine the brandy, Cointreau, and lemon juice and shake vigorously. Twist the lemon peel into the prepared glass and strain the cocktail over it. Serve immediately.

Lemon Twist

A lemon, or any citrus, twist is the colorful zest of a fresh lemon without any of the bitter pith attached; it should be 2 to 3 inches long. Twist it over a drink to release the zest's essential oils.

Tasting Your Cocktail

A bartender's trick to tasting a drink is to insert a straw with your thumb covering one end into the drink and extracting a small amount. Taste and determine whether something is needed to perfect the drink.

Here goes: This is the perfect drink. It's simple. It tastes like a drink, not a piece of candy or a fruit bomb. So many cocktails try too hard to make up for their lack of balance and purity. Rum, lime, sugar—that's all.

Says Ti, "The first time I ever had a Daiquiri, it was as mind-boggling as the first time I had quality sushi, which tasted pure, clean, and like the sea. I couldn't get enough. I've had the same problem with Daiquiris."

Think it's a girly drink? JFK and Ernest Hemingway didn't think so. The shame of it all is that it is hard to find a well-made Daiquiri. Most bartenders don't even know what you're talking about and even after you tell them you want it on the rocks you often end up with a frozen strawberry Daiquiri placed in front of you. Ugh!

It was invented in a small Cuban mining town named Daiquiri, in the late nineteenth century by American engineers who ran out of gin. With guests expected soon, they substituted the readily available rum. The locals took to what señor *was having, and the drink traveled back to America with the engineers.*

It is important to use the right rum in specific cocktails. The Daiquiri uses light rum, which is clear and dry. Dark rum is aged for five to seven years, and is a key ingredient in drinks like the Mai Tai and Whoa, Nellie! Spiced rum is just that—rum spiced with cinnamon, nutmeg, vanilla, and other flavorings—and is used in Orgeat Punch.

Following are the three best versions we know. The first is the original, the second was Hemingway's favorite, and the last is a variation for the adventurous.

The Original Daiquiri

When muddling limes, you should be able to get a good 1 to 1½ tablespoons of juice to make this drink properly. If your limes seem a bit dry, use another slice or two. Be careful not to muddle too much, as the juice will become bitter.

Daiquiris traditionally are served on the rocks, but Bar Chef Lu serves her Daiquiris at the Swizzle Stick with crushed ice, giving them an almost frozen effect. But, heaven forbid, not made in a blender.

Makes 1 cocktail

2 lime wedges, or more as needed
1 sugar cube
1½ ounces light rum
Up to 1 teaspoon Simple Syrup (*page 139*),
optional, for balance if limes are bitter

Muddle the limes and sugar cube in a rocks glass to break down the sugar and lime. Add the rum and stir well. Taste the drink and adjust with a little simple syrup as needed. Add ice to fill the glass to the rim and serve.

The Papa Doble

Maraschino liqueur is a clear cherry liqueur with no relation to the bright red cocktail cherries of the same spelling. Seek it out at your liquor store to make this drink properly.

Makes 1 cocktail

1½ ounces white rum
¼ ounce maraschino liqueur
½ ounce grapefruit juice
¾ ounce Simple Syrup (*page 139*)
¾ ounce lime juice

Combine all the ingredients in a cocktail shaker and shake vigorously. Strain over crushed ice into a rocks glass and serve immediately.

Adventures in Daiquiris ☀

This is a variation on the classic Daiquiri, with the optional addition of Southern Comfort. It's a bit sweeter than the usual and is served with crushed ice so it looks like what we in New Orleans call a "sno-ball" (or snow cone for you other folks). When you muddle, the grit of the sugar helps break down the skin of the lime wedges to release their essential oils.

Makes 1 cocktail

2 lime wedges, or more as needed
1 sugar cube
1 ounce dark rum
1 ounce Southern Comfort
Simple syrup (*page 139*), optional,
for balance if limes are bitter
Crushed ice

Muddle the limes and sugar cube in a rocks glass. Add the rum and Southern Comfort and stir well. Taste the drink and adjust with simple syrup as needed. Add ice to fill the glass and serve.

Pisco Sour

A clear to pale amber grape brandy made from Muscat grapes in Peru and Chile, pisco is strong and tart. The Pisco Sour is refreshing yet tongue loosening. Both countries claim its invention, though Peru rightly holds that title. Proportions of all the ingredients should be experimented with and argued over as they do in Peru and Chile. Any bar that stocks pisco or, better yet, lists the Pisco Sour on its drink list is a bar after our own hearts—like Loa at the International House Hotel in New Orleans. There are many brands of pisco, but we prefer Aba.

Makes 1 cocktail

1½ ounces Pisco Aba
¾ ounce fresh lemon juice
1 ounce Simple Syrup (*page 139*)
2 drops Angostura bitters, plus 2 dashes for garnish
1 large egg white

Combine the pisco, lemon juice, simple syrup, 2 drops bitters, and egg white in a cocktail shaker with ice and shake vigorously. Strain into a small cocktail glass or a sherry glass and shake the remaining 2 dashes bitters on top. Serve immediately.

Pegu Club Cocktail

This cocktail was a 1900s invention of the Pegu Club in the then British colony of Burma. When Audrey Saunders opened her own smashing bar in New York in 2005 and named it the Pegu Club, we thought we had better try that drink.

We marveled at Audrey's deft hand in remaking New York's famed Bemelmans Bar a few years before, having been longtime fans of both Bemelmans and the adjacent Café Carlyle. We read about Audrey's legendary intensity, her drive to get each cocktail right and to understand and respect its history and derivation. To prove this point we spent hours late one night with Audrey and Dale and Jill DeGroff tasting Ramos Gin Fizz after Ramos Gin Fizz because she wanted to know how we New Orleans restaurant brats remembered it.

At today's Pegu Club, there are house-made bitters on the bar with various people's names on them. This is a place with dedicated cocktail aficionados and damn good drinks.

See the Source Guide (*page 141*) for ordering orange bitters.

Makes 1 cocktail

2 ounces Tanqueray gin
¾ ounce fresh lime juice
¾ ounce Marie Brizard orange curaçao
1 dash Angostura bitters
1 dash orange bitters

Fill a Martini glass with ice. Combine all the ingredients in a cocktail shaker filled with ice and shake vigorously. Strain the cocktail into the chilled Martini glass. Serve immediately.

Lallis and Ti talking in Manhattan

Blood and Sand

Good scotch-based cocktails are hard to come by. Fear not; this is a well-balanced, stunning drink. Dramatic as its name, too, if served with a flamed orange peel.

The flamed orange peel is King Cocktail Dale DeGroff's signature touch. One night at Commander's Palace he showed general manager Steve Woodruff how to squeeze the peel of an orange ever so slightly while lighting it with a match or lighter to create a mini sparks show. It's surprising and very debonair and cool the first time you see it. Twist it above the drink and then drop it in.

Makes 1 cocktail

¾ ounce scotch
¾ ounce Cherry Heering
¾ ounce Italian sweet vermouth
¾ ounce orange juice
1 flamed orange peel, optional

Combine the scotch, Cherry Heering, vermouth, and orange juice in a cocktail shaker with ice and shake vigorously. Strain into a Martini glass, garnish with a flamed orange peel, if using, and serve.

Mix One Drink at a Time

Almost all of our cocktail recipes call for mixing one drink at a time. While there are some, such as Bloody Marys and Margaritas, that can be made by the pitcherful, take the time to mix each cocktail separately for proper balance and value.

If you do serve cocktails frequently, invest in several individual serving-sized shakers.

Bubblies and Fizzes

While Champagne and other sparkling wines are perfect on their own, especially when toasting those special occasions, they also pair well with other carefully chosen ingredients. Fizzy, nonalcoholic mixers like ginger ale or ginger beer turn a pour of vodka into a cocktail.

It's up to you whether to use that special bottle of French Champagne with a capital *C* when mixing cocktails, but we find that sparkling wines from California, Spain, and elsewhere are more than just fine.

French 75 Number 1

hat will they wear tonight? What will they order? We often traveled with our aunts as young girls and we thought a fancy hotel bar was a mysterious and wonderful place. If we "behaved," we were allowed to go along. At least before dinner.

A French 75, she ordered. The drink was a bubbling golden liquid in a tall Champagne flute reflecting the red cherry and looked like a mini fountain with an endless flow of bubbles. Wow, we thought, she looked glamorous and happy drinking it—and so very sophisticated.

Named for a powerful but reputedly very smooth French 75 millimeter cannon that was said to have helped win World War I, this drink could be used as a weapon of war—or love.

This version uses Cognac instead of the gin that is popular in New Orleans establishments.

Makes 1 cocktail

1 ounce Cognac
¾ ounce Simple Syrup (*page 139*)
½ ounce fresh lemon juice
½ to 1 ounce Champagne

Fill a Champagne glass with ice and set aside. In a cocktail shaker, combine the Cognac, simple syrup, and lemon juice and shake vigorously. Discard the ice from the glass, strain the mixture into the prepared glass, and fill to the top with Champagne. Serve immediately.

French 75 Number 2

There are two schools of thought about what goes into a French 75. For us, it's an easy choice: gin in the spring and summer, and Cognac or brandy in the fall and winter. Here's the summer version.

Makes 1 cocktail

1 ounce gin
¾ ounce Simple Syrup (*page 139*)
½ ounce fresh lemon juice
½ to 1 ounce Champagne

Fill a Champagne glass with ice and set aside. In a cocktail shaker, combine the gin, simple syrup, and lemon juice and shake vigorously. Discard the ice from the glass, strain the mixture into the prepared glass, and fill to the top with Champagne. Serve immediately.

Moscow Mule

The Moscow Mule was first served in a cold copper mug with two mules as a promotion for John Martin's new product, Smirnoff vodka. This cocktail took off when it was first served to the see-and-be-seen crowd at the Cock 'N Bull in Los Angeles, circa 1939. Now people knew what to do with vodka: mix it with something else.

In the nineteenth and first half of the twentieth centuries, ginger ale was spicy with a strong ginger flavor. Today's ginger ale is not as gingery and just won't do for this drink. Seek out a strong ginger beer such as Blenheim's Hot Hot Ginger Ale or Blenheim's Ginger Beer, both of which have quite a kick—like a mule.

Makes 1 cocktail

1½ ounces vodka
1½ ounces ginger ale or ginger beer

Combine the vodka and ginger beer in a highball glass filled with ice and stir. Serve immediately.

The Right Glass

Here in the land of cocktails, the culture of cocktails extends beyond the drink. It's about the entire ritual: Setting out the toasted pecans in grandmother's Baccarat crystal bowl, catching a breeze on the front porch, sharing recipes with friends over a tray of Sidecars. And choosing the right glass for each cocktail is essential. A straight-up Martini loses its cachet when it's not served in a Martini glass. Though there is certainly an appropriate glass for every drink, determine the glass that gives you the most enjoyment. Remember, the original cocktail (the Sazerac) was served in an eggcup, or *coquetier*.

No one expects your home bar to be as well stocked as a restaurant's, but having some appropriate glassware makes cocktail drinking a better experience. If Martinis are your thing, then purchase some stemmed glasses. For drinks served on the rocks, use 6- to 8-ounce rocks glasses, also known as Old-Fashioned glasses. Tall drinks made with juices or mixers call for 8- to 12-ounce highball glasses.

Although we call for specific glasses in each recipe, feel free to use what you have on hand.

Melon Coolia

Cool breeze. Rocking chair. Good friend. Melon Coolia. Let all ingredients rest.

Makes 1 cocktail

1 ounce Midori liqueur
1¼ ounces Simple Syrup (*page 139*)
1¼ ounces Sour Mix (*page 139*)
2 ounces Champagne
1-inch cube of honeydew melon
1 maraschino cherry without stem

Combine the Midori, simple syrup, sour mix, and Champagne in a cocktail shaker with ice and shake. Strain into a Champagne flute. Garnish with the honeydew and cherry on a cocktail pick.

Rock Star

When you order this drink, of our invention, at the Swizzle Stick Bar at Café Adelaide in New Orleans, we give you sunglasses to wear and a rock star scarf.

Makes 1 cocktail

2 ounces Maker's Mark
2 ounces citrus-flavored energy drink, such as SoBe
1 splash cola

Combine all the ingredients in a rocks glass, stir, and add ice. Serve immediately.

Champagne Cocktail

Atimeless classic originally made popular in 1862. A Champagne Cocktail is one of the rare instances when the wide mouthed, shallow glass is used with Champagne instead of the tall, thin flute. Flutes can be used if you don't have coupes. Using a sugar cube, rather than simple syrup, is classic as well.

Ladies, if we escort you to Table 8 at Commander's Palace, we hope you're ready to say "I do." More couples have gotten engaged at Table 8, a romantic corner nestled in the Coliseum Room, than throughout the entire restaurant. Champagne and Champagne Cocktails are de rigueur for such occasions. Unless the lady says no. Then it's "Check, please."

Makes 1 cocktail

1 sugar cube
6 dashes Angostura bitters
Chilled Champagne, to fill the glass
Lemon twist, for garnish

Place the sugar cube in the bottom of a Champagne glass and drop the bitters onto it. Fill the glass with Champagne and garnish with the twist. Serve immediately.

Winter
Warmers

Sometimes the world and the weather are just too, too cold. It's times like these—the first bite of autumn, on a blustery winter afternoon, when your team is losing the Super Bowl, at the end of a long week—that a warming drink is your only hope to set things right. These are the occasions to pull out those Irish coffee mugs from the back of the cabinet and mix these drinks.

In New Orleans, warm, coffee-based drinks like Café Brulot or Irish Coffee are often served at the end of the meal in place of a plain cup of joe.

And who says a chilled drink can't warm you up? A Widow's Kiss will change your mind.

Café Pierre

We have long loved Café Brulot, Irish Coffee, and other coffee-based drinks, but Café Pierre is a family favorite. Ti was once going to do a radio interview about our family tradition at Commander's Palace of serving flaming coffee tableside. She knew the histories of many drinks, but not this one. So Ti called her mother, Ella, who giggled and said, "Oh, your Aunt Claire, Uncle John, and Aunt Adelaide were eating at Brennan's in Dallas one night and decided to invent a flaming coffee drink. The captain who was assisting this foray into mischief was named Pierre."

Be sure to use heatproof glassware that can handle hot beverages, such as Irish coffee glass mugs. At our restaurants we use wineglasses. They will be very hot once the coffee has been added to them. Pierre's solution was to fold a linen napkin in such a way as to make the perfect "mitts" for guests to hold the stem of the glass.

Makes 2 drinks

2 tablespoons sugar
1 lime wedge
2 ounces brandy
2 ounces Kahlúa
2 ounces Galliano
2 cups hot strong black coffee
½ cup Sweetened Vanilla Whipped Cream (*page 140*)

Place the sugar in a shallow dish. Wet the rims of two heatproof all-purpose wineglasses with the lime wedge. Roll the wet glass rims in the sugar. Holding each glass by the stem, and turning it over a low flame, melt the sugar until it is the color of caramel.

Divide the brandy, Kahlúa, Galliano, and coffee between the two glasses and stir. Gently spoon a thick layer of whipped cream into each glass and serve immediately.

Goodnight, Lally ♔

L ally loves vanilla. Lally works late. One late night Lu concocted this coffee drink for Lally just before closing time at Café Adelaide.

Bright yellow Licor 43 has forty-three ingredients in it, one of which is vanilla. Part of the fun here is making the glass look like a snow globe by coating it with sugar. During a snowstorm, this is the nightcap of choice. It's fun for us, of course, to think of people everywhere whipping up Goodnight, Lallys.

Makes 1 cocktail

2 teaspoons superfine sugar
1 ounce Licor 43
1 ounce Martell Cordon Bleu or
other medium-bodied Cognac
6 ounces very strong, hot black coffee
1 large dollop Sweetened Vanilla
Whipped Cream (*page 140***)**

Place the sugar in a shallow dish. Lightly wet the outside of a large, heatproof wineglass or glass coffee mug with water and roll through the sugar to lightly coat. Combine the Licor 43, Cognac, and coffee in the glass and stir to combine. Top off with the whipped cream and serve immediately.

Café Brulot

*B*efore preparing this tableside cocktail at the restaurant, we dim the lights in the dining room. The captain then pours orange-red flaming coffee into the glass down a long orange peel spiral dotted with cloves that he holds up as high as his head—quite the scene-stealer. We use a Sterno at the restaurant; at home, prepare this in a 2½-quart saucepan.

Makes 2 drinks

1 lemon
1 orange
2 dozen whole cloves
1½ ounces triple sec
1 ounce brandy
2 cinnamon sticks
1½ cups strong black coffee

Peel the lemon, in one continuous motion so that the peel is in a long spiral, over a heatproof bowl in order to catch the juices. Discard the pulp or reserve for another use. Repeat with the orange. Insert the cloves into both peels at 1-inch intervals. Spear both peels at one end with the tines of a large fork and set aside.

Heat the triple sec, brandy, and cinnamon sticks in a saucepan. When hot, carefully ignite the mixture with a long-handled match. Holding the fork with the citrus peels, ladle the flaming brandy down the peels.

Gradually add the coffee, pouring it around the edges of the saucepan to extinguish the flames. Ladle the coffee into 2 heatproof coffee cups or Irish coffee mugs and serve immediately.

Irish Coffee

Irish coffee was popularized in America at the Buena Vista Café in San Francisco. In 1952 bar owner Jack Koeppler enlisted Stanton Delaplane, a famous travel writer, to perfect the recipe originally served at Ireland's Foynes Flying Boat Terminal, where American and European seaplanes landed during World War II. Irish barman Joe Sheridan, who invented the drink to warm the weary travelers, was inspired by one group who traveled eighteen hours, arriving exactly nowhere, having had to turn back due to poor weather. The Flying Boat Terminal is now Shannon International Airport.

We were raised in a large Irish clan, and when Lally's father, John Brennan, and our uncle Dick hosted their annual St. Patrick's Day luncheon for about seventy of their Irish pals at Commander's, we knew three things:

1. Lunch would merge with dinner.
2. These handsome Irishmen would try to outdo one another by wearing the most outlandish green and green plaid jackets and pants. Why this affront to fashion occurred, we do not know. It was our duty to act appalled and theirs to look ridiculous.
3. The only way to get them out of the dining room around 5:00, to prepare for dinner, was to entice them onto the patio with promises of Irish coffees.

Makes 1 drink

2 ounces Irish whiskey
4 ounces hot, strong black coffee
1½ teaspoons brown sugar
½ teaspoon white crème de menthe
1 dollop Sweetened Vanilla Whipped
Cream (*page 140***)**

Fill a coffee mug or heat-resistant glass with hot water to warm it. Discard the water. Combine the whiskey, coffee, sugar, and crème de menthe in the mug. Gently spoon the whipped cream on top and serve immediately.

Bourbon Hot Toddy

This is just what the doctor ordered to take the chill off and bring comfort when you're feeling a little low. Our parents were known to dispense tiny portions of this to us when we had bad colds: "One drop for you, three sips for me."

Makes 1 cocktail

2 ounces bourbon
1 teaspoon honey
6 ounces hot water
1 cinnamon stick
3 dashes nutmeg

Combine the bourbon and honey in a brandy snifter. Add the hot water and stir with the cinnamon stick. Garnish with the nutmeg and serve immediately.

Widow's Kiss

The distinct flavors of each ingredient make this perfect for a mid-winter evening, even though it's a chilled drink.

Makes 1 cocktail

1½ ounces Calvados
¾ ounce Green Chartreuse
¾ ounce Bénédictine
2 dashes Angostura bitters

Fill a Martini glass with ice to chill. Combine all the ingredients in a cocktail shaker with ice and shake vigorously. Discard the ice and strain into the chilled glass. Serve immediately.

Not Your Average Cup of Joe

New Orleans is a serious coffee town and coffee port. Visitors have long found our coffee to be strong. It may be strong, but, because it has chicory mixed in, it contains less caffeine than most cups of joe.

Chicory is a holdover from the Civil War days, when it was added to extend coffee. The chicory roots are kiln-dried, roasted, and added to the coffee, giving it a distinct, almost bitter, taste that we prefer.

Summer
Refreshers

Sure you can always offer cold beer and chilled white wine to your guests in the dog days of summer, but nothing beats the heat like an icy summer cocktail. Warm weather cocktails should not be oversweet as is too often the case. Well-made mojitos should have just a hint of sweetness or a subtle mint flavor when combined with their respective rum and cachaça.

Classic summer refreshers like Mai Tais and Daiquiris are all about that ever important balance of spirits and other ingredients. Try some of our new classics such as the Belladonna and Tequila Mockingbird 2.

Belladonna

All restaurants and bars have their favorite regular customers. Kim Dudek is one of ours. She invented this drink and has been drinking it at Commander's Palace and Café Adelaide for years. We named this drink the Belladonna after her luxurious and popular day spa and salon in New Orleans.

Blood orange vodka is less sweet than other orange- or citrus-flavored vodkas. While you can make it with regular orange-flavored vodka, the drink will not taste the same.

Makes 1 cocktail

**2 ounces Charbay Blood Orange vodka
or other citrus-flavored vodka
1 ounce Cointreau
1 ounce Sour Mix (*page 139*)
½ ounce cranberry juice
1 lime wedge, for garnish**

Fill a Martini glass with ice to chill. Combine the vodka, Cointreau, sour mix, and cranberry juice in a cocktail shaker with ice and shake vigorously. Discard the ice from the glass and strain into the chilled glass. Place the lime wedge on the rim of the glass and serve immediately.

Negroni

Our family was introduced to the Negroni at a small café on Rome's Via Veneto by the most dapper gentleman we can remember, Charles Gresham. He was an interior decorator and a dear friend with impeccable style who lived, like our Aunt Adelaide, in a different world. If he said Negronis were elegant, they were. And are.

A favorite Charlie Gresham story goes like this: One day he arrived at Aunt Dottie's home to help her decide which color to paint the house exterior. Upon arrival in the midafternoon—dressed impeccably in a three-piece suit with a cane and pocket watch on a chain—he requested a folding table, a chair, and a pitcher of Negronis. He then set up shop in the little park across from Dottie's house. He sat there alone, staring and sipping for about an hour and a half. He then rang the doorbell, said "Pink," and left. She painted the house pink.

Makes 1 cocktail

1 ounce Campari
1 ounce sweet vermouth
1 ounce gin

Combine all the ingredients in a rocks glass and stir. Add ice to fill the glass and serve.

Royal Bermuda Yacht Club

There really is a Royal Bermuda Yacht Club, dating back to the mid-1800s, and this is the house drink. British fellows, you know. The drink appears in an early edition of *Trader Vic's Bartender's Guide*. And for proper homage to the club, use a Bermuda rum, like Gosling's Black Seal or Bacardi 8. Falernum is a clear, flavored syrup that ranges from 5 to 11 percent proof. It has a subtle sweet and tart taste that adds to rum-based cocktails.

Here's an example of the importance of balance when mixing cocktails. While testing this recipe, the amount of Falernum was off; the drink was so austere, it nearly didn't make it into this book! Moral of the story: Always taste your cocktails before serving them to guests.

Makes 1 cocktail

2 ounces Bermuda rum
¾ ounce fresh lime juice
2 teaspoons Falernum
2 dashes Cointreau
1 lime wedge, for garnish

Combine the rum, lime juice, Falernum, and Cointreau in a cocktail shaker with ice and shake vigorously. Strain into a stemmed sherry glass, garnish with the lime wedge, and serve immediately.

Americano

A version of the Negroni without the gin.

Makes 1 cocktail

1½ ounces Campari
1½ ounces sweet vermouth
Splash club soda
Flamed orange peel (*page 60*), for garnish

Combine the Campari and vermouth in a rocks glass, add the club soda, and stir. Add ice to fill the glass and garnish with the flamed orange peel. Serve immediately.

To some people, Trader Vic probably sounds like a fictional character; to cocktail lovers he is a hero figure; and to our family he was a good friend and a genius restaurateur.

We grew up hearing the story about Vic showing Ella his Quonset hut restaurant. He had struck on a theme and he was going all-out. Who knew what Polynesian food was anyway? He used to say, Ella recalls, "If you don't serve the same thing as your competitors nobody can compare prices. You serve grilled shrimp, I serve Polynesian Island shrimp."

When Ella visited Vic in California, he wanted to show her everything, complete with an aerial view from his plane, which was a very big deal in those days. Ella was pregnant, Vic was smoking, Ella and others were drinking, and the plane was unpressurized. We still think our brother and cousin Alex (the son she was carrying) turned out okay, but that adventure could explain a few things. Such dangers were yet to be discovered.

Mai Tai

The legendary Trader Vic, genius restaurateur and creator of exotic or "tiki" drinks, invented the Mai Tai. Here's his version.

Just as a great chef can invent a dish in his head and know how it will taste, Vic could do the same with cocktails. One day in 1944, while hanging out at his restaurant, he decided to create the best rum drink ever. As he was finishing, some friends from Tahiti arrived, and he allowed them the first taste. They proclaimed "Mai tai, roe ae!" which is Tahitian for "Out of this world, the best."

It is important that this drink not be just pink and sweet. Dress it up if you like. At Trader Vic's each one came with a gardenia floating in it.

Makes 1 cocktail

1 ounce gold rum
1 ounce dark rum
½ ounce lime juice
½ ounce orange curaçao
¼ ounce Simple Syrup (*page 139*)
¼ ounce Orgeat Punch (*page 16*)
1 sprig mint
1 wooden skewer with a wedge of orange
and pineapple and a maraschino cherry

Combine the rums, lime juice, curaçao, simple syrup, and orgeat punch, in a cocktail shaker with 1 cup ice. Strain into a highball glass filled with a cup of ice. Garnish with the mint sprig and the skewered fruit and serve.

Bruce McAlpin's Mai Tai 👑

Bruce McAlpin is a dear friend with whom we have shared many a misadventure. He has such a warmth and grace combined with a naughty twinkle in his eye, we think Trader Vic himself would be okay with this more elaborate version of the Mai Tai. When you gather on the porch to watch the sunset after a day on the beach, followed by naps and showers, Bruce serves his drinks in fun-colored cocktail glasses on a matching tray.

Bruce's Mai Tai has nine ingredients! He doesn't even tell you that—you have to pry it out of him. He wouldn't want you to think he had gone to a lot of trouble. How gauche would that be!

Makes 1 cocktail

1 ounce dark rum
1 ounce light rum
½ ounce Orgeat Punch (*page 16*)
½ ounce Simple Syrup (*page 139*)
Juice of 1 lime
1 ounce pineapple juice
1 ounce orange juice
¼ ounce grenadine
1 maraschino cherry without the stem, for garnish

Mix all of the ingredients, except the cherry, in a cocktail shaker with ice. Strain into a highball glass filled with ice, garnish with the cherry, and serve immediately.

Tequila Mockingbird 2 👑

The tale of a drink's invention in three parts:

Part I: One night at the Commander's Palace bar, we tell Bryan Batt, our childhood friend, Broadway actor, and all-around beloved character, that we are hard at work on a cocktails book. He says he's had in mind a great drink name for years, and we must invent a drink and call it the "Tequila Mockingbird." We laugh so loud it is quite unladylike.

Part II: Lu creates a drink and says, "Ti, try this." It's good, but Ti asks her to add two dashes of Angostura bitters. She does. The drink is perfect. We are prouder than proud.

Part III: When all-knowing Doc Cocktail comes into the Swizzle Stick Bar, we offer our new invention to get his praise. He informs us that there is already a drink called the Tequila Mockingbird but that it's not very good and he can't wait to taste ours. He loves it and proclaims it the Tequila Mockingbird 2.

Makes 1 cocktail

2 ounces Reposado tequila
1 ounce limoncello
1 ounce fresh lemon juice
2 drops Angostura bitters
½ ounce Simple Syrup (*page 139*), or more to taste
1 lemon twist, for garnish

Fill a Margarita glass with ice to chill and set aside. Combine the tequila, limoncello, lemon juice, and bitters in a cocktail shaker filled with ice and shake vigorously. Add the simple syrup, adding more if necessary. Strain the drink into the chilled glass, garnish with the lemon twist, and serve immediately.

Redheaded Stepchild ♕

There are no redheaded stepchildren in our Irish family. Lots of redheads though, and we all cheer when a redheaded baby is born into the family. Adelaide was a redhead, and so are Dottie and Ti; and—coincidentally enough—so is Lu. The cayenne rim makes this drink a redhead, too.

This is an example of not only a delicious original cocktail, concocted by Lu one creative afternoon, but also how an inventive rim flavors a cocktail. This sugar-cayenne rim adds eye appeal and, more important, a zesty kick.

Makes 1 cocktail

1 teaspoon superfine sugar
1 teaspoon cayenne pepper
1 lemon wedge
2 ounces peach brandy
1 ounce Calvados
1 ounce orange juice

Combine the sugar and cayenne pepper on a saucer and mix well. Wet half of the rim of a chilled Martini glass with the lemon wedge and dip into the sugar-cayenne mixture. Set aside.

Combine the brandy, Calvados, and orange juice in a cocktail shaker filled with ice and shake vigorously. Strain into the prepared glass and serve immediately.

Caipirinha

This is the Margarita of Brazil. The critical ingredient is cachaça, a sugarcane brandy with a unique taste, somewhere between a silver rum and white tequila. Look for brands such as Carninha 51, Pitú, Velho Barreiro, and Ypioca.

Crush, or muddle, the lime with the sugar to release the essential oils from the lime rind along with the juice. Serve it over crushed ice, which keeps you from guzzling this potent cocktail. Show restraint; you'll thank us in the morning.

Makes 1 cocktail

1 lime half, quartered
1 sugar cube
2 ounces cachaça

Place the lime wedges and sugar cube in the bottom of a rocks glass and muddle to extract the juices. Add the cachaça and stir. Add ice and serve immediately.

Cachaça Swing

This drink is distinguished by its beautiful deep red color and the unique flavor of cachaça, the rumlike spirit extracted from sugarcane. Cachaça is ubiquitous in Peru and Brazil as the main ingredient in the Caipirinha.

Makes 1 cocktail

1½ ounces cachaça
¾ ounce Falernum
½ ounce crème de cassis
1 drop Peychaud bitters
Splash soda water

Combine the cachaça, Falernum, crème de cassis, and bitters in a highball glass and stir well. Add the soda water and stir. Add ice and serve immediately.

Mojito

The semitropical weather in New Orleans is ideal for serving island-inspired drinks. While we love a Mint Julep, a Mojito gives that same mint kick in a drink that's cleaner and lighter, and it's made with white rum, not bourbon. Don't overdo it with the mint: a little goes a long way.

Makes 1 cocktail

2 tablespoons loosely packed crushed fresh mint leaves
1 ounce Simple Syrup (*page 139*)
½ ounce fresh lime juice
1½ ounces dark rum, such as Cruzan
1 sprig fresh mint or 1 lime wedge, for garnish

Combine the mint leaves and simple syrup in a rocks glass and muddle the mint with a spoon to break the leaves and release the essential oils and flavors. Add the lime juice and rum and muddle again. Fill the glass with ice, garnish with a sprig of fresh mint or a lime wedge, and serve immediately.

Stoli O Delicious ♛

This drink, the creation of Mike Manganaro, native New Orleanian and bartender at the Swizzle Stick Bar, won a national cocktail competition. The contest rules—create a drink with Stolichnaya Orange and make it delicious—led to the name, "Stoli O Delicious."
Omit the simple syrup if you prefer a less sweet cocktail.

Makes 1 cocktail

1 ounce Stolichnaya Orange vodka
½ ounce peach schnapps
½ ounce limoncello
½ ounce fresh lemon juice
½ ounce Simple Syrup (*page 139*), optional

Combine all the ingredients in a cocktail shaker with ice and shake vigorously. Strain into a chilled Martini glass and serve immediately.

Our parents, along with Pete Fountain, Al Hirt, Chris Owens, and a host of other locals, figured out early on that if they worked together as ambassadors of New Orleans, they would all get their fair share. They formed their own highly effective, if unofficial, tourism marketing commission. If a travel writer was coming into the restaurant, Ella or Adelaide or Dottie or John or Dick would call down the street to Pete, Al, and Chris and let them know. Everyone made it their business to make it a night that the writer never forgot.

Paloma

This cocktail is similar to the popular Salty Dog, but uses tequila instead of vodka, with a bit of orange curaçao to round it out.

Taste your grapefruit juice to determine how much simple syrup to add. The sweeter the juice, the less syrup you'll need.

Makes 1 cocktail

1 lime wedge
2 tablespoons kosher salt or sea salt
2 ounces Ruby Red grapefruit juice, preferably fresh
1½ ounces Reposado tequila
½ ounce orange curaçao
¼ ounce Simple Syrup (*page 139*), or to taste

Rub half of the rim of a Margarita or Martini glass with the lime wedge and dip into the salt. Using a clean cloth, wipe any excess salt from inside the glass and set aside.

Combine the remaining ingredients in a cocktail shaker with ice and shake vigorously. Strain the cocktail into the prepared glass, add ice to fill, and serve immediately.

Kahuna Juice

In the South, everyone has his or her own version of Planter's Punch or some other rum fruit punch; some are better than others. This is our salute to the craziest, most loving, prank-prone crowd of cousins and friends and relatives we grew up with in New Orleans and spent summers with on the Mississippi Gulf Coast.

We gathered at an oak-shaded park among a smattering of cabins on the beach next to a seafood shack and oyster bar we once owned called the Friendship House. The cousins—Alex, Brad, Tommy, Dickie, Daly, Ralph, Cindy, Lauren, and Brenne—and friends would water-ski, sail, jet-ski, swim, bowl, roller-skate, play baseball, fish, crab, tell ghost stories, play cards, and on and on. Often a batch of fruit punch was mixed up outdoors in a large ice chest. One night when the boys taste-tested a bit too much, one of them spent the entire night on land in his water skis and life vest, having been told by an older friend that the Big Kahuna would sleep outside and guard his Kahuna juice. Needless to say, the cousin obliged and awoke covered in ants, which had been attracted to the juice and rum.

Makes 1 cocktail

1 ounce light rum
1 ounce orange juice
1 ounce pineapple juice
½ ounce amaretto
½ ounce crème de banane
Splash of grenadine
½ ounce dark rum

Combine all the ingredients except the dark rum in a cocktail shaker with ice and shake vigorously. Pour the contents of the shaker, including the ice, into a highball glass. Add the dark rum, do not stir, and serve immediately.

Eye-Openers

*N*ot everyone drinks at breakfast? News to us. As little girls we'd go to work with our family for Breakfast at Brennan's. It could be Sunday brunch or 9:00 a.m. on Tuesday, but the dining room was magical to us. Waiters in their green or red jackets (depending on the time of year) darted about as though in a finely choreographed ballet. One balanced a tray of plump poached eggs under marchands de vin sauce and baked oysters casino on the half shell, the piquant and creamy smells arriving before the food. Another flamed Café Brulot, transforming chicory coffee and brandy into a cologne thick with cloves.

People sipped Sazeracs and frothy Ramos Gin Fizzes that looked like shaken milk to us. Waiters served Mint Juleps in shiny, sweating goblets and layered Pousse-Cafés with the layers of bright colors one on top of the other.

It was magic.

Breakfast had never been like this before. It still is. At Commander's Palace brunch, there are balloons of every color centered on the tables like party hats to let customers know they can relax and enjoy New Orleans cocktails even early in the day.

Brandy Milk Punch

Our favorite Mardi Gras drink is Milk Punch. It is a perfect daytime drink, for any brunch or breakfast—or enjoyed on your Mardi Gras float.

Make a batch the night before serving. Put it in an empty plastic milk jug (all the better for transporting onto your parade float), and then let it, as we say, "marinate" overnight in the refrigerator. It just tastes better.

One year, long before anyone we knew had a cell phone, our dear friend Celia Slatten, a tugboat magnate, became irked when our float's Milk Punch supply ran out before the parade even began to roll. Her butler, who was helping Celia load her beads to be thrown, brought out a strange contraption none of us had ever seen before, a foot-long mobile phone. She called Ella at Commander's Palace, just a block off the parade route, and when we passed near the restaurant, a sea of white toques in the crowd passed gallons of Milk Punch up to the float.

Makes 1 cocktail

2 ounces brandy
1 ounce Simple Syrup (*page 139*)
½ teaspoon pure vanilla extract
1½ ounces milk
Freshly grated nutmeg, for garnish

Combine all the ingredients in a cocktail shaker with ice and shake vigorously. Strain into a rocks glass filled with ice. Garnish with a light dusting of freshly grated nutmeg and serve immediately.

Brandy Alexander

There are two schools of thought on the Brandy Alexander: those who consider it an eye-opener and make it with heavy cream or milk, and those who enjoy it made with ice cream and served as a dessert or after-dinner drink. The breakfast version is first, followed by the late-day recipe.

Makes 1 cocktail

1½ ounces brandy
2 ounces heavy cream
1 ounce dark crème de cacao

Combine all the ingredients and 1 cup of ice in a blender. Blend on slow speed until frothy and well combined. Pour into a rocks glass and serve immediately.

Makes 1 cocktail

2 ounces brandy
1 ounce dark crème de cacao
1 cup good-quality vanilla ice cream

Combine all the ingredients in a blender. Blend on slow speed until just thick. Pour into a brandy snifter and serve immediately.

Absinthe Suissesse

What a civilized way to greet the day. Start brunch with this classic cocktail, followed by Eggs Sardou, and then brown sugar baked apples for dessert, and the world looks pretty good.

Makes 1 cocktail

1½ ounces Herbsaint or Pernod
½ ounce Orgeat Punch (*page 16*)
½ ounce half-and-half
1 large egg white

Fill a rocks glass with ice and set aside. Combine all the ingredients with ½ cup ice in a blender and blend until frothy. Discard the ice from the glass. Pour the drink into the glass and serve immediately.

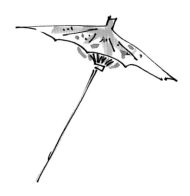

Lu's Bloody Mary ♛

Lu's Bloody Marys are so popular that she makes them by the pitcher at the Swizzle Stick. We suggest you do the same for brunch. Make the mix the night before and keep it refrigerated until ready to serve.

Lu adds pickled okra or green beans to hers, but try cherry tomatoes, cocktail onions, pimiento-stuffed olives, celery, or whatever else may suit your fancy.

Makes 8 cocktails

2 teaspoons Creole seasoning
One 32-ounce bottle V-8 juice
6 tablespoons Worcestershire sauce
1 teaspoon cayenne pepper
1 teaspoon garlic powder
½ teaspoon Crystal hot sauce, or more to taste
9 lemon wedges
2 cups vodka
8 lime wedges
Garnishes, as described above

Place the Creole seasoning on a saucer.

To make the Bloody Mary mix, combine the V-8, Worcestershire, cayenne pepper, garlic powder, and hot sauce in a pitcher and stir well to combine. Refrigerate if making ahead.

Just before serving, wet half the rims of eight highball glasses with 1 of the lemon wedges and dip the rims into the Creole seasoning. Wipe the insides of the glasses with a clean cloth and set aside.

Divide the vodka equally among the eight prepared glasses. Fill each glass halfway with the Bloody Mary mix, stir well, and add ice. Place 1 lemon wedge and 1 lime wedge on the rim of each glass and garnish as desired. Serve immediately.

Jamie Shannon's Bloody Mary

We believe that New Orleanians have fewer regrets at the end of our lives than people who live elsewhere. We love and live fully, sometimes with abandon. Although most of us know how to hold our liquor rather well, there are inevitable occasions when the arrival of morning is shocking. But as the boys in the kitchen say, "If you hang with the big dogs, you got to get up and go with the big dogs."

No one embodied this better than Jamie Shannon, our beloved chef at Commander's Palace for twelve years, who died at age forty in 2001. He missed out on much because of his early death, but in his forty years Jamie packed more into life than most who live twice as long. Some of that big living can be cruel the next morning and remedies abound. Aunt Adelaide had her vapors remedy; Jamie had his Bloody Mary.

We picture Jamie standing in the Commander's kitchen early on a Saturday or Sunday morning. Six feet, three inches tall and imposing, but with the gentlest drooping Irish eyes, his perfectly neat long ponytailed hair still wet at the tips, and a part-grin part-grimace that hid very little. The ultimate "big dog" would never let on that he was hurting as he went about his business with a glass of strong iced chicory coffee always at hand, even though we knew he'd rather be drinking his Bloody Mary.

Jamie developed his own Bloody Pepper mash, a hot sauce–like condiment, that he kept in a giant wooden barrel. At various times, he added more peppers and vinegar to keep it going, and he tended to it like an old lady with a rose garden, always tasting and tinkering. Jamie's Bloody Mary is the one to end all Bloody Marys.

Makes 1 cocktail

1½ ounces vodka
1 teaspoon prepared horseradish
1 teaspoon or 2 splashes Worcestershire sauce
2 dashes Pepper Mash (*page 114*) or 4 dashes
Crystal hot sauce and 2 dashes Tabasco
½ cup V-8 or tomato juice
Creole seasoning, either seafood or meat
1 pickled pepper and pickled okra, skewered on a
sugarcane stick or cocktail pick, for garnish

Fill a tall glass two-thirds full with ice cubes and add the vodka, horseradish, Worcestershire, hot sauce, and vegetable juice. Cover with a shaker and shake, then let rest in the shaker. Wet the rim of the glass and place in the Creole seasoning, coating the entire rim of the glass. Pour the drink back into the glass and garnish with the pepper and okra.

If you like extra seasoning, season the top of the drink with fresh cracked pepper and kosher salt.

Pepper Mash

S ure, you can buy pepper mash, but making it is easy and you can control the amount of heat. But plan ahead. While the preparation takes just a few minutes, the salted peppers have to marinate for two days, and then the mash has to sit for a month or two before it's ready to use.

Use one kind of pepper, such as cayenne, or a combination, adding sweet red peppers if you want less heat. While some people strain their mash, Jamie didn't, preferring the chunky, rustic texture. When the mash is ready, you can put some in nice bottles with corks or lids to give as gifts. And be careful when handling hot peppers—do not touch your eyes.

Makes about 1 quart

1½ pounds hot peppers, such as cayenne,
jalapeño, habanero, or a combination
1 cup kosher salt
3 cups white vinegar

Remove the stems and roughly chop the peppers. Place in a stainless bowl and sprinkle with the salt. Stir and cover with plastic wrap. Place in a cool, dry area for 2 days, stirring every 12 hours.

Add the vinegar to the peppers and puree with a hand blender or food processor. Place in a sterilized glass jar, cover with a clean lid, and refrigerate.

As time goes by and you have an excessive amount of ripe peppers, again wash, remove the stems, chop, and add to the jar. When the jar is totally filled, remove the sauce, puree, and place in a clean jar and age until it reaches the desired flavor, at least 2 months.

Angostura Restorer ♛

*B*itters were invented to settle the stomach—and they do! Unless, of course, you take yours with a whole lot of whiskey.

Even the most devoted cocktail drinkers, like us, take some nights off. Many a restaurant guest thinks we are having a cocktail with them, when, with a wink and a nod, the bartender serves us one of these instead.

This was created by our legendary New Orleans barman and friend Michael Manganaro.

Makes 1 drink

2 ounces soda water
2 ounces tonic water
2 ounces 7-Up
6 dashes Angostura bitters
1 lemon wedge

Combine the soda, tonic water, 7-Up, and bitters in a highball glass, stir, and add ice. Squeeze the juice from the lemon wedge into the drink and drop the wedge into the glass. Serve immediately.

The After
Party

We watched the six guests from Kansas all night. We don't know what they enjoyed most, the restaurant or one another's company. These folks were happy to be together. The captain said something about a reunion of sorts. The men—no, gentlemen—stand each time the ladies leave and return to the table. We love that, and their mothers for teaching them. They don't do it reluctantly, but gladly—a badge of honor from a different era. They laugh loud. They're easy with one another; these are old friends. They push back in their chairs and roll their eyes with pleasure after passing a fig and white chocolate tart around the table. They don't want their evening to end. Neither do we.

"Stan, you know what we want to send table thirty-one?"

"Café Pierre is coming up, ladies. On the house, right?"

"On the house."

As Stan prepares the coffees, bouncing flames dance from one glass to the other, and the whole dining room stops to watch the show. We approach table thirty-one, "Stan, showing off again?"

The guests laugh and we chat a few minutes. We say as we walk away, "They don't have coffee like that in Kansas, do they?" Their laughter follows us across the room.

Strega Salute

This first pousse-café is a simple one, with just three layers. It was concocted by Swizzle Stick bartender Michael Manganaro for a Strega liqueur bartenders' contest. He won the contest—and a trip to Rome.

Makes 1 cocktail

¼ ounce grenadine
¼ ounce green crème de menthe
¼ ounce Strega

Pour the grenadine into a small liqueur glass. Next, carefully add the crème de menthe by gently pouring it over the back of a spoon so it remains separate from the grenadine. Repeat with the Strega. Serve immediately.

Pousse-Café

Only the most gracious bartender can keep a smile when a pousse-café is ordered. Making this fancy drink takes time, serious bartending knowledge, and a steady hand. Having originated in France, it was all the rage in swanky bars and hotels in New Orleans in the 1840s. It means "to push coffee" and was meant as a drink to go with after-dinner coffee.

A pousse-café is a spectacular, showy drink with colorful layers of liqueurs. To make one successfully you have to know the relative weight of each liqueur so the layers remain separate. The "heaviest" liquid—the liqueur with the least alcohol content—goes in first. Barkeeps use the straight end of a narrow spoon, never touching the side of the two-ounce straight-edged glass.

T-Shot

*A*nother of Michael's winning combinations.

Makes 1 cocktail

¼ ounce white crème de cacao
¼ ounce Tia Maria
¼ ounce Bailey's Irish Cream
¼ ounce half-and-half

Pour the crème de cacao into a small liqueur glass. Next, carefully add the Tia Maria by gently pouring it over the back of a spoon so it remains separate from the crème de cacao. Repeat with the Bailey's Irish Cream and then the half-and-half. Serve immediately.

Grasshopper

A classic cocktail that tastes like chocolate mint ice cream with a kick.

Makes 1 cocktail

1 ounce green crème de menthe
1 ounce half-and-half
½ ounce white crème de cacao

Combine all the ingredients in a cocktail shaker with ice and shake vigorously. Pour the contents, including the ice, into a rocks glass and serve immediately.

Elizabeth Taylor 👑

Lu likes a challenge when it comes to creating new cocktails. Anyone can dream up a colorful drink that looks pretty in a glass, but how about one that looks *and* tastes good? Lu had in mind to invent a drink the exact color of Elizabeth Taylor's eyes. She succeeded in looks, flavor, and balance.

Makes 1 cocktail

1½ ounces citron- or lemon-flavored vodka
1 ounce cranberry juice
½ ounce triple sec
½ ounce blue curaçao
½ ounce fresh lemon juice

Fill a Martini glass with ice to chill. Combine all the ingredients in a cocktail shaker with ice and shake vigorously. Discard the ice in the Martini glass. Strain the cocktail into the glass and serve immediately.

Close the doors — the little room

Just Close the Doors ☼

There is a room at Commander's Palace—the Little Room—where private parties of sixteen or fewer are held. It has a balcony overlooking Lafayette Cemetery #1. We don't know how to explain it, but so many who enter the small doorway cross into a parallel universe—one where they misbehave, shall we say.

Our late beloved maître d' of forty years, George Rico, would come running to one of us and whisper about what was going on in the Little Room, asking if they should be kicked out. Since we usually knew the guests involved—or their children—we would often say, "Just close the doors." Once, we did have to ask a group to leave the restaurant and never return, but they have been known to sneak back in under assumed names. We know—and they know we know. We do not, however, let them sit in the Little Room.

To make this drink, shake the cocktail shaker longer than usual, until it is very frosty on the outside and small ice crystals form in the cocktail itself.

Makes 1 cocktail

1 ounce Chambord
1 ounce Licor 43
1 fresh raspberry, for garnish
1 lemon twist, for garnish

Place the Chambord and Licor 43 in a cocktail shaker with ice and shake vigorously for double the usual amount of time. Strain the cocktail into a brandy snifter or sherry glass and garnish with the raspberry and lemon twist. Serve immediately.

The John Brennan Stinger

John Brennan's drink of choice was a Stinger. Come holiday time it seemed he always had one in hand. Handsome, rather dashing really, Lally's father was a pilot in World War II. We learned years later the Stinger was a favorite with the flyboys back in the big one. Who knew? At Commander's the Stinger will always be the John Brennan Stinger.

Makes 1 cocktail

1½ ounces crème de menthe
1½ ounces brandy

Fill a rocks glass or brandy snifter with ice to chill. In a cocktail shaker with ice, combine the crème de menthe and brandy and shake vigorously. Discard the ice from the glass. Strain into the glass and serve immediately.

Bananas Faster

Get it? Make Bananas Faster by putting them in the blender!

Makes 1 cocktail

2 packed teaspoons dark brown sugar
⅛ teaspoon ground cinnamon
1 orange wedge
½ cup vanilla ice cream
2 ounces dark rum
1 ounce crème de banane
½ banana, peeled and sliced lengthwise

Combine 1 teaspoon of the sugar and the cinnamon on a saucer and mix well. Wet half the rim of a brandy snifter with the orange wedge and dip the rim into the sugar-cinnamon mixture to coat. Set aside.

Combine the ice cream, rum, crème de banane, banana, and the remaining teaspoon of sugar in a blender and blend on high speed until smooth, about 20 seconds.

Pour into the prepared glass and serve immediately.

Coupes de Milieu

During long, grand Creole suppers or luncheons in the earliest days of New Orleans, a midmeal palate refresher was often served. The coupe de milieu was made with liqueurs and fruit that were frozen, or as frozen as something with that much alcohol could be. Some thought the purpose was to "make a hole in your stomach," or make room for the remainder of the meal. One example is oranges that are first roasted in brandy or claret-spiked syrup and then frozen.

With the advent of our tasting menus at Commander's Palace, we have revived the coupe de milieu. Try it between courses or even as dessert.

Strawberry Sling

This coupe de milieu and the one that follows were created by Chef Danny Trace at Café Adelaide and the Swizzle Stick Bar.

Makes 4 cocktails

½ cup strawberries, pureed in a blender
1 ounce fresh lemon juice
1 ounce Simple Syrup (*page 139*)
1 ounce soda water
1¼ ounces Tanqueray gin

Combine all the ingredients in a cocktail shaker with ice and shake to chill. Strain into a cordial glass.

Brick gutters line the streets in the French Quarter, making for curbs that sit up higher than usual. Our curbs are a great place to stop, sit, and take in all the goings-on. Even though we're actually sitting on the curb, we call this pastime "sitting in the gutter."

One night in the early 1950s, while sitting in the gutter in the French Quarter, Ella introduced herself to the lovely couple sitting in the gutter next to her. They turned out to be restaurateurs Bernice and Mac McHenry of the famed Tail of the Cock in Los Angeles. They became lifelong friends and loved to reminisce about how they met sitting in the gutter.

Watermelon Caipirinha ♛

Makes 6 cocktails

½ lime, quartered
2 teaspoons sugar
2 ounces cachaça
1 cup watermelon pieces, pureed in a blender

Muddle the lime and sugar together in a shaker. Add the cachaça and watermelon puree. Cover with ice and shake to chill. Strain into cordial glasses and serve.

Captain's Banana Smoothie ♛

Commander's Palace executive chef Tory McPhail is responsible for the next four recipes. Proceed with caution.

Makes 4 cocktails

5 teaspoons sugar
½ ounce fresh lime juice
1 ounce vodka
1 ounce spiced rum
1 medium banana

Place all the ingredients in a blender with 2 cups ice and blend on high speed. Divide among 4 tall glasses and serve.

Caribbean Painkiller 👑

Makes 4 cocktails

2 ounces orange juice
1 ounce fresh lime juice
2 ounces coconut rum
1½ ounces vodka
2 ounces pineapple juice
A pinch or ⅛ teaspoon grated nutmeg, for garnish

Place all the ingredients except the nutmeg in a cocktail shaker with ice and shake to chill. Divide among Tom Collins glasses, garnish with nutmeg, and serve.

Tequila Mango Freeze 👑

Makes 6 cocktails

2 lime wedges
3 tablespoons sugar
3 ounces Añejo tequila
1¼ cups mango cubes, fresh or frozen
8 teaspoons sugar
2 ounces fresh lime juice

Wet half of the rims of six highball glasses with the lime wedges and dip the wet rims in sugar.

Combine the tequila, mango, sugar, lime juice, and 2 cups ice in a blender and mix at high speed until smooth. Divide among the glasses and serve.

No one remembers why but at the old Café Lafitte, now known as Lafitte's Blacksmith Shop, a blind alcohol tasting contest was often held. The crowd of locals held something of a drinking "salon" with great conversation and lots of carrying on. They would line up all the different liquors in shot glasses—gin, rum, tequila, scotch, bourbon, etc. You had to drink and then name each one. When we asked Ella why they did this, she shrugged with a smirk and said, "To see if we could." Apparently no one ever could—except the then editor of the Times-Picayune, *who nailed it every time.*

Eggnog Coupe de Milieu 👑

𝒫erfect for holiday dinners and parties.

Makes 6 to 8 cocktails

2 medium eggs
1 cup heavy cream
⅛ cup sugar
Pinch of ground cinnamon
½ cup Southern Comfort
⅛ teaspoon pure vanilla extract
Grated nutmeg, for garnish

Place the eggs, heavy cream, sugar, and cinnamon in the top half of a double boiler or in a stainless-steel bowl. Place the pot or bowl on top of a double boiler with simmering water. Whisk until the mixture is thick and frothy, 6 to 8 minutes. Pass the mixture through a mesh strainer into a bowl, and place in the refrigerator until chilled like custard. When cold, finish by whisking in the Southern Comfort and vanilla. Divide among chilled shot glasses and garnish each with freshly grated nutmeg.

Pairing Cocktails with Food

We've hosted and attended scores of wine and food dinners and events. We love to drink wine and grew up with it at our dinner table before it was common in other American households. As we became more and more interested in cocktails, we wondered about pairing them with food, thinking perhaps that some cocktails might be better matches for certain dishes. Well, this was our "aha" moment.

During our rediscovery of the Daiquiri, the question arose of what to eat with this pristine cocktail. Soon after, at Café Adelaide we served a hot Daiquiri-painted snapper accompanied by a classic Daiquiri. It was unbelievably good; the lime and rum flavors permeated the fish. Jimmy Buffett may put down his Margarita for this.

Our quest wasn't over. We tried more cocktail and food matches that didn't work than those that did. In fact, although it's actually hard to ruin a food-and-wine pairing, cocktails and food are a much greater challenge. Still, when it works, pairing cocktails with food can be truly sublime.

First, decide whether the cocktail will complement the dish or contrast it. Consider the integral flavors found in the ingredients, where those dishes originated, and what liquors or liqueurs come from those areas. Caribbean foods and seafood pair beautifully with rums, which are native to that region. Pair a ceviche with a tequila-based cocktail; the tequila will cut through the rich, tender seafood and complement the bright citrus marinade. Think sturdier, dark liquors with steak and heavier meat dishes, like scotch drinks with rack of lamb or an Old-Fashioned with breast of duck. Pair rum drinks with vinaigrette-dressed salads.

Desserts call for a sweet cocktail—nothing harsh or too sugary—perhaps with fresh berries or chocolate cake.

Then there's the entertainment factor of pairing food with cocktails! Think of it as a parlor game of sorts. Get out your cocktail shakers, imagine flavor combinations, taste, and pair! Don't like that one? Well, taste and try again! Surprise your friends by hosting a cocktail pairing dinner party.

The cocktail can be your best friend when entertaining. It is a forgiving soul: it likes to come out and play; it wants to make new friends. What's more, a well-made cocktail, by dint of the multiple flavors from its components, has hidden layers just waiting to be awakened by the flavors of a particular dish. When the drink is better with the dish and vice versa, you have hit a home run.

Another tip is not to serve food that is complicated. Allow the cocktail to highlight the flavors of the dish and accent the sum of the various parts.

Keep in mind, too, that cocktail pairings are personal matters—you may not like what the next person does. Don't be intimidated, just keep mixing it up, and you will have your own Whoa, Nellie! moments.

The Cocktail Pantry

Simple Syrup

Simple syrup is nothing more than a combination of sugar and water, usually boiled until the sugar dissolves. Instead of boiling hers, Lu adds hot tap water to the sugar. It dissolves just the same. Keep a jar in the fridge and use it for making lemonade, sweetening iced tea, and, of course, in cocktails.

Makes 2 cups

2 cups sugar
2 cups boiling water

Place the sugar in a heatproof container, add the boiling water, and stir until dissolved. Let cool to room temperature.

The cooled syrup will keep, refrigerated, in a jar or container for up to a month.

Sour Mix

Also known as bar mix, sour mix is a combination of lemon (sometimes lime) juice with simple syrup and is used in many drinks.

Makes 3 cups

2 cups fresh lemon juice
½ cup water
½ cup Simple Syrup (*see above*)

Combine all the ingredients and keep, refrigerated, in a jar for up to a month.

Sweetened Vanilla Whipped Cream

I f possible, try to find cream that has not been ultrapasteurized.

Makes 1 cup

½ cup cold heavy cream
1 tablespoon confectioners' sugar
¼ teaspoon pure vanilla extract

Place the cream in a medium bowl and beat with an electric mixer at medium speed or by hand until thick and frothy. Add the sugar and vanilla and continue to beat until soft peaks form, being careful not to overmix. Though the cream will hold its peaks for several hours in the refrigerator, you should use it immediately.

Source Guide

Regans' Orange Bitters
> Visit www.buffalotrace.com/giftshop.asp or call
> 1-800-654-8471.

Fee Brothers Orange Bitters
> Visit www.surfasonline.com/products/22796.cfm
> or call toll-free 1-866-799-4770.

Peychaud's Bitters
> Visit www.buffalotrace.com/giftshop.asp or call
> 1-800-654-8471.

Index